Postmodern
Children's Ministry
Ministry to Children in the 21st Century

Ivy Beckwith

Postmodern
Children's Ministry

Ministry to Children in the 21st Century

Ivy Beckwith

ZONDERVAN™

GRAND RAPIDS, MICHIGAN 49530 USA

Postmodern Children's Ministry
Copyright © 2004 by Ivy Beckwith

Youth Specialties Books, 300 South Pierce Street, El Cajon, CA 92020, are published
by Zondervan, 5300 Patterson Avenue SE, Grand Rapids, MI 49530

Library of Congress Cataloging-in-Publication Data

Beckwith, Ivy, 1954-
  Postmodern children's ministry : ministry to children in the 21st
century / by Ivy Beckwith.
    p. cm.
  ISBN-10: 0-310-25754-9 (softcover)
  ISBN-13: 978-0-310-25754-7 (softcover)
  1. Church work with children. I. Title.
  BV639.C4B38 2004
  259'.22--dc22

                                                              2004008752

Editing by Carla Barnhill
Proofreading by Laura Gross and Kristi Robison
Cover design by Burnkit
Interior design by Sarah Jongsma
Printed in the United States of America

09 • 10 9 8

This book is dedicated to my parents,
Rose and Irv Beckwith, who birthed me, fed me,
clothed me, educated me, and supported me
even when they didn't approve of me.

Acknowledgments

There are individuals and groups of people that in their own ways made this book possible. First, thank you to my friends and former colleagues: Tim Conder, Tony Jones, and Doug Pagitt. Thanks guys for sharing your lives and your friends with me. Without you I never would have discovered the world of Emergent nor found my community with these thoughtful and interesting men and women.

Second, I say thanks to the Children's Ministry volunteers and families of Colonial Church and Solomon's Porch. You have given me the freedom to experiment with the budding concepts and ideas found in the following pages, offering constructive ideas and forgiving me for my failures.

And last, but perhaps most important, I thank the children of Colonial Church and Solomon's Porch. Every week you teach me more and more about who you are and what you need. And every week you inspire me with your unique and interesting ways of following Jesus. Without you, this book never would have been written.

—Ivy Beckwith

Contents

Over the last 25 years the role of the Children's Ministry professional has come of age. The Minister to Children is often the second or third staff person a church hires. North American churches take seriously the need to provide spiritual nurture and care for their children and families. This is a good thing.

In the last 15 or so years, the discipline of children's religious education has developed gradually into a respected discipline of church ministry. Graduate schools of religious education have developed masters or certificate programs in childhood religious education. Lay programs and conferences for the continuing education of children's ministry professionals have proliferated and compete with one another for attendees. Parachurch organizations designed to support the children's minister have sprouted all over the continent. This is a good thing.

Church curriculum publishers, representing both the evangelical and mainline streams of American Protestant churches, help to mold this trend by putting more and more of their design and development dollars into publishing children's religious education materials and resources. The shelves of Christian bookstores are lined with books designed to help adults teach children the Bible, and many larger or chain stores have Christian education departments and Christian education specialists whose sole job is to work with the resources coming from these publishers. This is a good thing.

I have been an eyewitness to and a benefactor of this rise in respect and prominence of the church's ministry to children. I've worked in large evangelical churches as the

Director of Children's Ministries. I've worked for several curriculum publishers editing and marketing these new church curricula and resources. I've spoken and taught at national and regional children's ministry conferences, holding workshops on everything from establishing classroom discipline to helping adults understand the emotional ins and outs of 10-to-12-year-olds. And I've seen good things happen both in my own church ministries and in others. I rode the wave of this children's ministry growth trend for all it was worth.

Now I think it's time for a change. Toward the end of my tenure in the Christian publishing world, I heard many children's ministry professionals talk about the need to make their children's ministries "fun." One of the publishers for whom I worked briefly marketed their children's curriculum as "Funday School Curriculum." Please believe me—I'm not against fun. I like to have fun, and I don't want children to grow up viewing church participation as a dour experience. The learning experiences we provide for children should be appealing, engrossing, and creative. But I am concerned that all this emphasis on making our programs fun is eclipsing what I think the church should be about in its children's ministries, the spiritual formation of children.

When I left the publishing world to head back into local church ministry, I thought this trend might dissipate, but instead it has only become stronger. I frequently read the children's ministry message board on a church growth-related Web site, and once a completely flummoxed church planter posted a question about what to do with all the children who were coming to his new church. The children were almost equal in number to the adults who were attending. Another church planter advised the original poster to find two volunteers to watch the children and to instruct the volunteers to think of children's ministry as "a birthday party with a Bible."

At a meeting of large-church children's pastors, a woman commented on the pressure she felt from her church leadership to continually provide bigger, better, and glitzier programs for the children. I commented that perhaps that was not really what the children wanted nor what was needed to facilitate spiritual formation. She said in response that if she didn't provide those kinds of programs, no one would come. Families would choose to attend churches that did offer these types of children's programs.

Somewhere in our sincere quest to help children know and love God and live a life in the way of Jesus, we've lost our way. Somehow, in spite of all the good things happening in the church's ministry to children over the last two decades, we've forgotten what spiritually shaping these young lives is really all about and how to do it. It's time for a change.

Not only has the church lost its way in its quest to spiritually form its children, but it is also facing monumental cultural change. With that comes the need to think seriously about changing how churches help families form their children's souls. I left the helm of a children's ministry at a megachurch because the sheer size of it made it impossible to run the children's program I'd imagined. I needed to do something different for a while. So I worked in the Christian publishing industry. I attended and spoke at Christian conferences and conventions all over North America. At one of these conferences I heard positive rumblings about postmodernism. It was at that conference that I first heard really smart people grappling with ideas about the church's response to the seismic cultural changes coming about in light of this different way of understanding the world.

With my intellectual curiosity piqued, I set out to educate myself on postmodernism. I read everything I could find both in books and on the Internet. The more I read, the more convinced I became that postmodernism was not an enemy of the church to be defeated but something that could lead the church into a new way of thinking and being. Responding to these ideas and worldviews could lead the church into a new place of cultural relevancy. I became convinced that if the church did not grapple with postmodernism and those whose thinking is shaped by this culture, the church was going to be in deep trouble.

At about the same time I decided to return to local church ministry. I accepted a job as a Minister to Children in a large suburban church. Surprisingly, I found myself in a church that was taking these issues of culture and change seriously. I found myself surrounded by new and old friends who were having exactly the same thoughts and discussions I was having. This led me to think pragmatically about all I'd been rolling around in my head. In what ways does the children's ministry of the church need to change in order to meet the needs of the emerging culture of the 21st century? What does it mean for a community of faith to take seriously its responsibility to spiritually nurture its children and families?

This book flows from my thinking, reading, and discussions with others having the same sense of things, as well as from some experimentation in my congregation and others. It is very much a work in progress, and yet when I share these ideas with pastors and children's leaders around the country, the ideas are met with a positive and thoughtful response. The time has come to open this discussion to a much wider audience. What follows is an attempt to do just that.

The broad theme of this book is the spiritual formation of children in our emerging and changing culture. It's an effort to ask what that might look like and how it might happen for the generation currently on its way to adulthood. It's a book for anyone concerned about the way the church views its children and its programs for children. In the next pages I look at postmodernism—how it's shaping our culture and shaping those who we attempt to introduce to Jesus.

Because people interested in ministry to children are not just thinkers, but doers as well, this book offers positive, real-life examples of fresh ways of thinking about and doing children's ministry. I talk to people about their ideas and experiments. I show you what other communities of faith are doing to meet spiritual formation needs in this changing culture and new generation—and their dreams and hopes for new, vibrant, and meaningful ways of leading children down the path of the gospel.

In a plenary session of a large convention, I spoke about ministry to children—its current state and the need for a creative and thoughtful paradigm shift in how we love and nurture our children's souls. My words then have much to do with what this book is about:

The church's ministry to children is broken. A cursory look doesn't reveal its brokenness. From the outside children's ministry looks healthier than ever. But it is broken. It's broken when church leaders and senior pastors see children's ministry primarily as a marketing tool. The church with the most outwardly attractive program wins the children and then the parents. It's broken when we teach children the Bible as if it were just another book of moral fables or stories of great heroes. Something's broken when we trivialize God to our children. It's broken when we exclude children from perhaps the most important of community activities: worship. It's broken because we've become dependent on an 18th-century schooling model, forgetting that much of a child's spiritual formation is affective, active, and intuitive. It's broken when we depend on our programs and our curriculum to introduce our children to God—not our families and communities. It's broken when we've come to believe that church has to be something other than church to be attractive to children. It's broken when we spend lots of money making our churches into playlands and entice children to God through food fights and baptisms in the back of fire trucks. And perhaps most importantly, it's broken when the church tells parents that its programs can spiritually nurture their children better than they can. By doing this, we've lied to parents and allowed them to abdicate their responsibility to spiritually form their children. A church program can't spiritually form a child, but a family living in an intergenerational community of faith can. Our care for our children is broken and badly in need of repair. Let's imagine together a new way, a new future.

one

The Millennial Child and Beyond

One morning several years ago I had a short but memorable conversation with the Missions pastor of the church where I was employed as the Director of Children's Ministries. We were discussing how people understand the concept of truth. My friend made the point that the purpose of evangelism is to convince people that the Good News of Jesus is true. But, he said, the time would come when the response to our attempts to convince will be, "Okay, it's true. So what?"

I was intrigued by his words, and in the intervening years they have come back to me over and over again. I believe that Western culture and those that the North American church hopes to speak to are in this "so what?" era. With this change comes a host of new challenges to the church's mission of evangelism and discipleship, such as battling relativism, searching for new paradigms of gospel proclamation, and rethinking our understanding of the Bible.

Those of us who've made careers out of children's and family ministry have had a lot of success and recognition over the last 25 years. We've become professionals. We have academic degrees in Christian Education or Spiritual Formation. We have heightened awareness of the importance of specializing in ministries to children and their families. We've helped proliferate a multimillion-dollar curriculum-and-resource-publishing industry. And we've helped seminaries and Christian colleges grudgingly admit that what we do is a legitimate educational discipline, that it involves more than providing cut-and-paste activities for children in the church basement while the adults get on with God's real business. Web sites and nonprofit organizations dedicated to helping us do our jobs better are growing and providing more and more resources. Children's ministry has its own national conferences, and we have our own celebrities. Megachurches hold large events to pass on the secrets of their success in children's ministry. And I'm sure somewhere in all this we've seen God work among the children and families we've been privileged to know. Children's ministry has come a long way since Henrietta Mears, the founder of Gospel Light Publications, mimeographed Sunday-school curriculum in her garage. We've moved out of the shadows and into the limelight of church ministry.

Yet continuing on this track will not meet the needs of the current generation and the generation to come. If we hope to have any effect on the spiritual formation of the children and families that come to our churches in the next 50 years, children's ministry cannot continue as we know it. We need to be thinking about new paradigms, new ways of doing what we're doing, and we need to be thinking about it right now. If we don't, we'll soon find that we've become irrelevant to the families who live in the changing culture. We'll be scrambling to figure out what happened to everything that looked so shiny and unstoppable at the end of the 20th century.

I began to see this need for a revisioning of children's ministry as I grew to understand the formidable cultural change swirling around us. I heard a speech by a New Testament professor from a prominent midwestern seminary who was speaking to educational ministry professors and teachers. He addressed the subject of postmodernism and the church's response to it. I remember two things from what he said that day. First, he said that those holding a postmodern worldview do not believe in the existence of absolute truth. This statement reminded me immediately of the conversation I'd had years before with that Missions Pastor: I realized that the belief in absolute truth was foundational to so much of Christianity that the postmodern resistance to the idea of absolute truth could be a rather significant problem for the church—we would need to figure out how to answer the "so what" question.

Second, he described a weekly Bible study for business executives that he led in downtown Chicago. He explained that he never went into these sessions armed with formulas and arguments to convince the people of the truth. Instead he simply shared stories of God with them and guided their discussion of these stories. He introduced God to the people and let them decide for themselves. I couldn't help but believe he was on to something. He was proposing a way of bringing people to faith that didn't have anything to do with cut-and-dried teaching methodology. The idea struck a chord in me that day and sent me on the path to where I am today.

The Modern Era

For the last several years, the term *postmodern* has floated around academic and theological circles. (The term is also used in many other disciplines—art, literature, architecture—but it means different things in each context.) Now it is part of the popular vernacular, and yet most of us don't really understand what it means. I'm no philosopher and don't have a philosopher's understanding of the abstract thinking behind the term, but I can tell you how I've come to understand it as a layperson.

In order to understand how something can be postmodern, first we need to understand how something can be modern. Think back to the European history and philosophy classes you had in college or graduate school. Most likely you studied something called the Enlightenment or the Age of Reason that came around 1700 A.D. This era is commonly thought to be the beginning of the modern era. (In light of the church's resistance to postmodernism, it strikes me as quite ironic that my Christian college had no qualms about requiring a course on the Enlightenment.) Your professors may have talked about how philosophies of modernity came about as a reaction to the more superstitious, mystical, and religious thought of the Middle Ages.

During the Enlightenment, men and women (though mostly men) began to discover they could exert some kind of control over their world and conquer parts of it. Life, it was discovered, was not just a serendipitous journey where everyone was at the mercy of circumstances outside of personal control. Machines were invented that could do some tasks better than human beings. And people were discovering that the human ability to reason and solve problems was a useful tool for taming and mastering the external world. Perhaps, the philosophers mused, humans could be the masters of their own destinies. The only things human beings needed to make the world better was men and women who learned how to think and use their innate talents and skills more effectively. If humans could uncover the mysteries of the world, then perhaps it was no longer necessary to believe in that all-knowing, all-seeing God of the Middle Ages.

Philosophers believed human beings could discover the absolute truth about reality within themselves and that if they thought long enough and hard enough about it, they could solve any problem the world had to offer, eventually perfecting the world and themselves. Many of the thinkers of the Age of Reason had little use for the God of the Bible.

Moderns believe in absolute truth and that all truth is objective. They believe that the final word on all things, the understanding of objective reality, is out there somewhere and humans can find it through our capacity for reason. This objective, absolute truth is not subject to the whims or perceptions of kings, rulers, priests, or cultures. An assertion is true if it accurately and objectively represents the independent, external world. All this knowledge is accessible for all humans; there is nothing we human beings can't know if we just put our minds to it and analyze the problem or the situation. There is nothing humans can't do or understand eventually. Modern thinking holds absolute faith in the rational capabilities of the human mind.

Modernity is scientific. The sciences with their hypotheses, theories, seeming objectivity, and ability to experiment and test for truth are held up as one of the best pathways to absolute knowledge and truth. Modernity prizes analysis. If we can just look at a problem from all sides and use all of our brainpower to figure out the causes and effects, we'll eventually be able to find a solution. The best way to think, then, is logically, linearly, analytically, and unemotionally. Because the world is making progress in a straight line toward something better, moderns are extremely positive and optimistic about the future.

In addition, modern thinking emphasizes the work and well-being of the individual over and against group and community life. Men and women are on their own in what they accomplish. Each individual is responsible for herself and has the right to make her own decisions and mistakes. Pulling ourselves up or making something of ourselves is more important than the needs or abilities of the greater community. So modernity has great faith in the individuals to grasp and understand the absolute truth about the way things are. Once that truth is applied to individual lives and societal problems in a logical and analytical way, the world will be on its way to perfection. We can think our way to a better life and a better world.

Over the last 300 years, this modern way of thinking has infiltrated our culture—Western culture in particular—so completely that few people have ever considered that it is not necessarily the only way of understanding the world. As the minds of each generation have been formed by this modern way of thinking, so too were the institutions of those generations, including the church. The modern church, therefore, holds to some of these same ideas: the belief that we must defend our faith with solid arguments and spiritual truths, the insistence on personal acts of faith, the idea that the only secure faith is one built on a foundation of absolute, unshakable truth.

The Postmodern Era

Postmodern literally means "after modern." So when we say we've moved into an age of postmodernity, we're saying that the modern age has passed and we've moved into a new paradigm, a new overall worldview.

But these kinds of cultural shifts are never easy—or quick. When the world was moving from the Middle Ages to the Age of Reason, not everyone got there at the same time. People didn't wake up on January 1, 1700, look at their calendars, and say, "Goodness! Look at that! We've moved into the Age of Modernity." These cultural changes, while tumultuous and significant, are gradual.

And that's where we are now. We find ourselves in a world slowly leaning toward postmodern but still populated by a lot of people who hold a modern worldview. This leads to conflict and to at least one popular misconception about postmodernism. Lots of speakers and writers like to use the word *postmodern* and generational monikers like *Generation X* or *millennial* interchangeably. They treat the postmodern worldview as a life stage that one will likely outgrow as maturity settles in.

While it's true that many people under 30 tend to think in postmodern ways, viewing the world through postmodern glasses cannot be chalked up exclusively to life stage analysis. Research shows that about 30 percent of Baby Boomers, 50 percent of Baby Busters (or Xers), and 60 percent of millennials have postmodern sensibilities. And although I am squarely part of the Baby Boom generation, I have carried around postmodern sensibilities my entire life. I just didn't know what to call them. I've never felt like I fit in with most Baby Boomers. I've thought and felt differently from most of my peers all my life—and now I know why.

But let's go back to those percentages for a minute. While I strongly believe this is not primarily a generational issue, it's worth noting that those with the strongest tendency toward a postmodern worldview are those currently labeled the Millennial Generation or Generation Y. These are the children we see currently in our churches. The

Millennial Generation has been described as those children born between 1980 or 1982 (social science makes no claims to being an exact science) and 2001. Some generational specialists believe the Millennial Generation ended on September 11, 2001.

So, sitting in your preschool classrooms every Sunday morning are a bunch of cute, curly headed postmoderns! Whether you agree with the postmodern way of thinking or not, ministering to these children demands that you understand their worldview.

Our world's new cultural and intellectual paradigm is truly a shift in the way human beings process information and in the way we view the external world. We're seeing a world where all the old certainties are dissolving. It's no wonder moderns are scared. Everything they've always hung onto as absolute truth, from our safety as a country to the way life is created, is being challenged and questioned. But it's happening. It's here. The church must understand it. And the church must deal with it.

Just as moderns believe there is discernable and knowable absolute truth and objective reality, postmoderns believe there is no overarching truth or ultimate ideal that explains and undergirds all of human existence. Postmoderns believe that reality or truth is always subjective. One's reality or truth grows out of one's perspective and life experiences. It is not imposed from the outside. Therefore, the modern idea of a metanarrative or a grand story that explains everything about the world is greeted with incredulity. J. Richard Middleton and Brian J. Walsh, authors of the book *Truth Is Stranger Than It Used to Be*, explain it this way:

> But if metanarratives are social construction, then like abstract ethical systems, they are simply particular moral visions dressed up in the guise of universality. And in falsely claiming universality

while being blind to their own constructed character, metanarratives inevitably privilege unity,
homogeneity, and closure over differences, hetero-
geneity, otherness, and openness. The result is that
all kinds of events and people end up being
excluded from the way in which the story gets
told. No metanarrative, it appears, is large enough
and open enough genuinely to include the experiences and realities of all peoples.[1]

Okay, that's a mouthful. Let's talk about it some. Big
stories whose intent is to explain truth or the meaning of
life all had to come from somewhere. That "somewhere" is
other human beings. All humans live in some sort of place,
country, community, or tribe. All humans live in a subjective context. No one can stand outside of her own reality.
Therefore, no big story can ever claim to be objective
because it cannot help but be colored by the prejudices,
beliefs, customs, and stories of the context from whence it
came. (Interestingly, missionaries have understood this for
years.) So postmoderns instead acknowledge that one's
beliefs and stories are local. They proclaim what is true for
that particular community or tribe. What is true for one
community is not necessarily true for another. Some postmoderns acknowledge that these big stories can be helpful
as explanations of personal reality while others condemn
them because the stories are seen as exclusive and closed
systems. But they can never be seen as objectively true.

This rejection of the universal truth of the metanarrative poses a problem for Christians because Christians
believe they have in their possession the only true metanarrative, the Bible. The story of God's plan for creation is
thought to explain all of life, reality, and truth. But it does
no good to browbeat people who don't believe in absolute
truth with the absolute truth they don't believe in.

Therefore we need to find new ways of looking at the Bible, new ways of talking about the Bible, and new ways of teaching what's in the Bible. And, frankly, this is really what this book is about. We'll deal with this issue more specifically in a later chapter, but for now let me quote a friend of mine on the subject of the Bible as metanarrative: "I like to think of it as the best metanarrative."

This lack of belief in a system of absolute truth translates into the postmodern idea that there is no common standard by which to measure, judge, or value ideas or opinions. What I believe is good, beautiful, moral, or normal is shaped by my environment, context, and culture. Other environments may have other standards as equally valid as the ones I hold. Let me give you two examples that illustrate the pervasiveness of this view in our culture.

A few years back the VH1 cable network aired a show called *The List*. The show revolved around a celebrity host and four celebrity guests. The premise was that the guests would determine the top songs or musical groups in a particular category such as "Best Love Song of All Time" or "Best Girl Group of the 1970s." Each guest listed three songs or groups fitting the category. After all the choices were revealed, each guest removed one of the picks from the list. Then the studio audience voted for their top three picks from the list, thereby determining the best of the category.

Now compiling "best of" or "top 10" lists is nothing new, but in the past, measurable criteria such as the number of records sold, amount of airplay, awards won, or concert grosses would have been used to determine what was best. But in the VH-1 world of *The List*, the only criteria used were the personal feelings, tastes, and preferences of the guests and the studio audience. No one seemed to mind that only subjective criteria were used to determine the winners. That's postmodern thinking.

The year 2000 brought the United States the first post-modern presidential election. In civics and history classes we've been taught that on Election Day Americans go to the polls and cast their votes, and one of the candidates gets more votes than the other and wins the election. What could be a more objective standard than counting votes? But on November 7, 2000, we awoke to a world where the system had broken down, and we had no clear winner. And as it turned out, the candidate with the most votes didn't win. We discovered that, depending on which side one was on, there were different ways to count votes and different ways to cast votes. Americans discovered that despite all the money, time, energy, and intellectual power put into election law and voting procedures, there is no objective criterion for determining who wins a presidential election that, statistically speaking, is a tie.

Nothing But the Truth

This lack of belief in objective standards or absolutes trans-lates into a form of relativism and a love of tolerance. Postmoderns, to a certain degree, say we have no right to judge the behavior, views, beliefs, or opinions of others because there is no standard outside of ourselves and our communities to tell us what is right and what is wrong. Any measuring stick is simply a human construction born from the biases and views of a particular group.

Moderns believe that all knowledge is good and allows humanity to progress toward something better. If we use our reason to the best of our ability, we can solve any problem and make the world better because there is noth-ing that human reason cannot eventually figure out. Postmoderns don't subscribe to this view that all knowl-edge is good, nor are they optimistic about the future. As they look out over their world, they don't see things get-ting better. They see continuing problems with racism, poverty, violence, sexism, and morality. They are skeptical about the ability of human reason to solve these problems. And they see the havoc human reason has wrought on the world in the forms of nuclear and biological technology.

Postmoderns believe that reason is not the only way to discover knowledge and truth. Emotions, intuition, and other less reasonable modes are valid paths as well. When I was in college and graduate school, an evangelical college ministry marketed an evangelism tool in the form of a booklet. The idea was for the "evangelist" to lead the "prospective convert" through the pages of the booklet that outlined the plan of salvation. After reading through the booklet, the evangelist was to challenge the person to accept Jesus.

Now there are many aspects of this evangelistic approach that would not appeal to the postmodern mind, but I want to focus on one in particular. At the end of the booklet is a drawing of a train. The locomotive, the engine that makes the train move, represents facts or truth. The locomotive of truth pulls a car that represents faith. The faith car is followed by the caboose of feelings. This illustration is meant to symbolize the process of faith: Once you know the reasonable truth (God loves you, you're a sinner, Jesus died for you, etc.), you will be led to have faith in God and accept Jesus as your Savior. A person has to believe these facts in order to become a Christian. Consigning emotion to the caboose is the warning that we can't trust our feelings and can't possibly know God through an emotional connection. A person holding a postmodern worldview would say that's a ridiculous assumption. Postmoderns put as much credibility into feelings, intuition, mystery, and other affective means of understanding as they do reason.

I once heard a well-known film critic dissect the Hollywood mind for his audience, and he expressed concern that the moral of many films made in the latter half of the 20th century was that a person should always follow his heart. These films tell us that our hearts will guide our choices so we don't need to be concerned about the consequences, he said. This critic was uncomfortable with the concept of personal truth and the idea of trusting emotions rather than human reason and objective standards of behavior. His discussion illustrates one of the points of conflict between the modern and the postmodern mind.

A Certain Line of Thinking

One of the popular criticisms of postmodernism is that it is illogical. To say there is no absolute truth, critics contend, is to state an absolute truth. A postmodern might respond, "So what? A premise doesn't necessarily have to be logical for me to believe it's true." Postmodern minds make interesting connections between data in what is sometimes called "loopy" thinking. The writers of *Seinfeld* understood completely this kind of thinking. Each episode consisted of several seemingly disparate plot lines that eventually crisscrossed each other and came together into a somewhat coherent (yet nonlinear) whole. In one episode the story was told in reverse chronology, starting at the end of the story and ending with the beginning.

A recent independent film, *Memento*, took this conceit to the extreme. It's the story of a man with short-term memory loss who's trying to avenge the murder of his wife—but the whole thing is told backward, starting with the murder and moving back through time. Along the way viewers are introduced to characters who we know will die because they were dead a few moments before.

The recent movie and Pulitzer Prize-winning novel *The Hours* jumps back and forth between time periods as it tells the story of three women deeply affected by the same Virginia Wolff novel. The novel is beautifully and compellingly written, and its nonlinear style allows the novelist some plot twists that could not have happened with a more straightforward narrative. *Seinfeld, Memento,* or *The Hours* couldn't have been created 25 years ago. Viewers would have found it ridiculous and illogical to play with the chronological, linear order of things.

Real Reality

Moderns believe it is possible to know what is real and what is not. Postmoderns aren't so sure about that. The line between reality and nonreality is blurred and porous, if there is even a line at all.

I have had the opportunity to attend several conventions held at the Opryland Hotel in Nashville, Tennessee. The huge, opulent theme hotel has gone to great expense to provide its guests with the experience of being in the lush environs of the Deep South. The central part of the hotel is built to create the world of the Louisiana delta. A river complete with boats winds its way through green and flowery vegetation, passing a street filled with shops designed to resemble New Orleans. The reality is that guests at the hotel are in a suburb of Nashville a few yards off of Interstate 40 and across the street from a Shoney's restaurant. But after spending a few days inside the hotel, it's easy to forget all that and instead enter the world of the Deep South. After a visit to the hotel I feel as though I've experienced the Bayou without ever traveling to the real place.

Disney spends millions of dollars simulating reality for children and families in their theme parks. Computer games and simulations are becoming more and more lifelike. Some people in Hollywood worry that computer-simulated actors might become so real that they will someday replace human actors. What is real and what isn't? How do we define real? Each day, advances in technology and science make these questions more difficult to answer.

Most of the children in our churches are immersed in this culture and are developing a worldview or way of thinking about things that reflects these postmodern tenets. Remember my earlier note that roughly 60 percent of millennials can be considered postmoderns? This percentage will probably be greater for the next generation, those babies who populate your nursery and toddler ministry. We need to realize that these children—known as adaptives (we'll talk more about them in a moment)—will not see the world the same way we do or even the way postmodern children in their early teens do. These children will not value the same things we value. These children will not understand the things that happen around them in the same way we do. They will not view concepts of truth and reality in the same way we do. This does not mean their outlook on life is wrong and must be changed. It's just different. If we are to minister to these children and their families, we have to understand their way of thinking and change our ways of doing things.

The Coming Generation

The current generation of children has been described as the most protected, most wanted generation. These kids are watched over. They grew up in car seats and seat belts. They all wear bicycle helmets. Their play is organized and regimented. They toddled around childproofed homes. Their teachers and caregivers are all screened with criminal background checks. Video cameras are installed in homes so parents can keep tabs on the baby-sitter. We do everything we can to ensure their safety.

Most of these kids were the result of planned pregnancies. The ease and prevalence of birth control enabled this generation of parents to have children when the time was right rather than have children foisted on them by a random act of nature. Many of these children are chosen children.

The millennials are cyberliterate and technology dependent. These kids were exposed to computers and high-tech gadgets from their earliest days. The Internet culture exposes these children to life around the globe. They can easily communicate with a child from Japan or get information on the Middle East. Exposure to more than a million Web sites reinforces the concept that truth is what one chooses to believe, not some objective standard that stands outside of us. Surfing the Net or hitting links from one screen or Web site to the next actually trains the child's brain to process information in narrative images. It fragments their thinking, which contributes to loopy or nonlinear thinking patterns. Computer usage also contributes to a child's ability to multitask. Every 13-year-old I know can instant message, e-mail, and surf the Web while watching television and talking on the phone. At a summer camp for older elementary school children, I asked how many had CD players, phones, computers, and/or televisions in their bedrooms. A high percentage of them owned two or more of these devices and had easy and somewhat unsupervised access to them. This is a generation of super-multitaskers who will move on quickly to new stimulation when they find boredom creeping in.

This generation is also shaping up to be passionately tolerant of differing opinions, cultures, and lifestyles. They believe in inclusion, not exclusion. Millennials have an emotional and intellectual openness not seen in previous generations, and they value highly personal freedom of choice. Millennials seem to believe intuitively that each person should do what is right for him; that each person should discover his own truth, his own story of the world, and live that out with integrity. This tolerance of other views and values is classically postmodern. These attitudes will be frustrating to those who hold to an objective standard of right and wrong. But this is the way most millennials think. Those of us who teach and love them will have to work hard at developing innovative ways to help them think through their own personal truths and values.

Generation Y is experience oriented. These kids find meaning and value in immediacy and in living in the moment. They want to experience something before they learn about it. Their mantra for life and learning and acceptance of views and values is "I want to try it." Only then will they decide if they like the experience or not. They've grown up with theme parks simulating every imaginable experience and event and with virtual reality computer games that transport them into fantasies and scenarios they could never access in real life. They want to use all their senses as they learn, and they want their learning environments to provide experiences, not just facts and formulas. They want to do in order to learn. And when it comes to developing a spiritual life—and they are spiritual people—they want to experience God, not just learn about God. They want mystery and mysticism. They don't just want to be entertained. Theologian Robert Webber quotes a youth director, who says,

> What appeals to this new generation is the cathedral and the stained-glass window. Take the pews out, let them sit on the floor, burn incense, have Scripture readings, lots of music, chants even, and have communion, and they say, "Wow, this is me."[2]

This generation is not quick to trust adults. Millennials have sensitive truth detectors and they can tell quickly if they are being conned. While they will give adults chances to prove themselves to be trustworthy; if they are let down by these adults they are unlikely to offer a second chance. They value integrity and honesty. They want people to be authentic with them. In *Kidscreen* magazine a 12-year-old girl said, "Goody-goody characters are very BORING. I like watching characters like Bart Simpson because it's funny when they get into trouble and then get themselves out of it. They are more real."[3] Because millennials are tolerant and accepting, it doesn't really matter what you are being real and authentic about—homework, troublemaking, religion—just as long as you are real and authentic.

Because they tend to trust themselves and their own opinions and truth, they don't put much stock in the directives of authority figures. As I speak with people who work with and teach millennial children, I hear consistently that these kids don't automatically give their respect to people who are older or in positions of authority. But if one wins their respect through being real and truthful, they will listen.

Even the "truths" about the millennials are open to interpretation. Neal Howe and William Strauss, the gurus of generational studies, say this generation mirrors the World War II generation, known popularly as "the greatest generation." They say millennials have the potential to be the most civic-minded generation since those of the early to mid 20th century.[4] Anecdotal evidence seems to bear out their thesis. Just weeks after the September 11 terrorist attacks, I heard a professor from a small college report about her students and their desire to make the world a better place. In talking with them about their futures, this professor found that they wanted to serve their country and help others. Doris Kearns Goodwin, the historian, talks of how one of her young adult sons joined the military after September 11 because he wanted to do something to make a difference for his country.[5] Recent interviews with the very young members of our armed forces reinforce this possible millennial desire to make our country and world a better and safer place. There are statistics that suggest that this generation values hard work but not necessarily career prestige; according to one survey more than 92 percent of millennials place high value on volunteer work.

But other researchers disagree. In his book *Growing Up Digital: The Rise of the Net Generation,* Don Tapscott suggests that this generation will be like Generation X only more so. He believes their independent values, their need for tolerance and inclusion, and their thirst for immediate experience and authenticity will actually act as impediments to their ability to be civic minded and other centered.[6] In reality the jury is still out on this aspect of the millennial generation. After all, many of them are still children whose identities are up for grabs. Richard Tiplady sums up these contradictions in a newsletter article:

> The "millennial" identity is not yet fully formed. They can be seen as currently a mix of "reactive" and "civic" (unlike Generation Xers, who are largely "reactive"). It is possible that millennials will be similar to Xers, but perhaps with more of a leadership orientation. We cannot yet say whether millennials will be a "civic" generation.[7]

What the experts do agree on is that children of this generation have the potential for living unselfish lives. We would do well to expose them to areas of service and mission in our churches.

Pollster George Barna notes that this generation is a spiritual one.[8] But simply being spiritual does not make one Christian. Millennials are open to the idea of God, but because of their acceptance of all points of view, they don't really know which God they believe in or want to believe in. They tend to have a pick-and-mix approach to spirituality, not necessarily buying into the complicated systematic theologies or step-by-step discipleship plans of the other modern generations. They are willing to accept certain tenets or values of Christianity, but they see nothing inappropriate about pairing these with ideas culled from Buddhism or other world religions. As postmoderns they don't believe that any one group or religion has the corner on truth. They are looking for an authentic spirituality or faith, one that reflects their stories and experiences, and that works for their lives.

The Adaptives

The personality of the millennial generation will become clearer as they move through childhood and adolescence and become young adults. What we do know about them and their postmodern worldview can help us shape our children's ministries for the next 10 or 15 years. But as I mentioned, we also need to be concerned about the generation coming after the millennials, the babies and toddlers in our churches. People who study generations name this group the "adaptives" or Generation Z. Nearly all of what we know about them is speculative because they are still too young to exhibit any group characteristics. But given the world they've been born into, we can make a few assumptions.

Each generation of the last 50 years has contained more and more members with a postmodern worldview. So it stands to reason that the adaptives will exhibit a greater percentage of those with postmodern sensibilities than even the millennials. So while the millennials will be leaving our spheres of ministry over the next 10 years, the adaptives will be with us for the next 20 to 25 years. This means that as we look to the future of ministry in our churches, we need to be serious about understanding this worldview and tailoring our visions, plans, and ministries toward the unique challenges of this generation.

The adaptives were (or will be) born after the terrorist attacks on New York City and Washington, D.C. They will never have the chance to see the twin towers of the World Trade Center dominating the New York City skyline. These children are born into a world where foreign-born terrorism is no longer an abstract concept or something that happens oceans away. These children will know a world of color-coded terror alerts and the anxiety produced by the stark reality that we could no longer believe we are safe from mass destruction in our own country. It is possible that they will live in a country of diminished civil liberties. This new national uncertainty may lead parents to become even more protective than the parents of millennials. Parents may be reluctant to travel by air or to foreign countries with these children, reluctant to let them take school trips to large cities, and may be more fearful for them each time they are out of sight. Parents may try to provide a safe world for their children in a real world that is increasingly unsafe. Emotionally, this could have a tremendous effect on this generation's ability to trust other people and themselves.

While early millennials were born into a world on the cusp of technological revolution, adaptives come into a world where amazing technology is commonplace and available in some fashion to most everyone. They live in a world where a digital device can record one's favorite television shows without commercials and then, based on those preferences, make assumptions about what other shows one might like and record those, too. They will view VHS tapes as relics in much the same way their parents view 8-track tapes as blasts from the past. They live in a world of DVDs and will never find it curious that the movies they rent and watch at home come packed with extra materials, directors' commentaries, and behind-the-scenes footage. It's likely they will never have to wait for their pictures to be developed. Their computers and handheld devices will be faster than anything the millennials have.

Rapidly changing technology will continue to allow these children and their parents to tailor life to their needs; you don't need to be home at a certain time to watch a particular television show, and cell phones let parents do a visual check-in with the kids. These children will be more techno savvy than their predecessors and, perhaps, more dependent on technology than earlier generations. New technologies may even redefine how we conduct relationships and how we teach children in all spheres of life.

Adaptives are born into a more ethically murky world than millennials. The tsunami of societal change brought on by postmodern sensibilities has made any pretense of certainty about ethical issues a precarious position to hold. The mapping of the human genome, debates about stem cell research, and strides made in cloning technology have fired up the age-old debate about the way life is created. These kids will grow up in a world hotly debating the nature of marriage and family. The sex scandals in the North American Roman Catholic Church send these children into a world where the traditional moral arbiters of society are seen as suspect and duplicitous. Like the millennials, the adaptives will need to be shown what a good life looks like, not simply taught moral lessons. Competing moralities and competing ethical systems will offer these children a wide variety of choices for making values-based decisions. Continued scientific and technological discoveries will make belief in the certainty of any kind of absolute truth a leap for these children.

Early millennials were born into a country in economic recession and then grew up during the go-go recovery and economic expansion of the '90s. They saw people not much older than themselves making millions and millions of dollars in dot.com IPOs. Some later millennials may continue to benefit from the economic harvest reaped by their parents during the boom years, but they face dimmer prospects for quick personal wealth.

Adaptives are born into a shaky national economy that—partly because of the threats of terrorism and war—wavers between sliding back into recession or moving into a strong, but curiously jobless, recovery. These children may not have the monetary advantages of their millennial predecessors. They may have to settle for state colleges and universities rather than the Ivy League. Vacations may not be as frequent or as lavish, and these children may live with the effects of a parental employment layoff or career change. Adaptives may not develop the expectations for large salaries and luxury lifestyles that their parents or early millennials did.

Adaptives come into a world where media continues to blur the line between reality and fiction, truth and untruth. More and more television programming is taken over by the reality genre purporting to show regular people acting naturally in contrived situations. But what's shown to the public are outrageous, salacious behavior sometimes engineered by the shows' producers. Journalism scandals at major newspapers call into question the truth of what is reported about world events. Filmmakers' special effects and computer-generated images are so real that we sometimes don't know if we are watching a live actor or a CGI creation. This generation will need to explore and answer questions about what is real and what isn't. And maybe, more importantly, the question: Does it even matter if it's real? This is a generation, even more so than the millennials, for whom the whole nature of truth as we've always known it and thought about it will be called into question.

As I said, during the last 25 years children's ministry in the church has gained respect. Like youth ministry before it, it has become a discipline, a specialization, something those training for church ministry aspire to do. And we've become pretty good at it. But the North American church stands at the crossroads, and those of us who work with children and families stand with it. We can continue on the path we're on, the one cleared by our ministry celebrities and parachurch children's ministry organizations. Taking that path will continue to garner us success for a while. But if we ignore or, perhaps worse, fight against the tidal wave of change taking place in our world and in our children, the respect and influence we've gained will come to a quick end. This is the path that will do damage to our children, our churches, and our faith.

The other path is uncharted. Some seminal, creative thinkers and practitioners have begun to clear the way, but the path is still overgrown with brambles and can lead us toward false turns. It's the path of embracing and understanding postmodern sensibilities, not fighting or denying them. It's the path of thinking creatively about bringing a discussion of faith and the Christian story to our children in both new and old ways. It's the path of rethinking how we help our kids experience the story, how we help our church communities and families experience the story with their children, and how we find in the story new and delightful and unsettling ideas about God and God's relationship to creation and the future.

Notes

1. Middleton, J. Richard and Brian J. Walsh, *Truth Is Stranger Than It Used to Be*, InterVarsity Press, 1995, 71.

2. Youth director quoted by Robert Webber "Faith: New Generation Is Looking Back," Uwe Sieman-Netto, United Press International.

3. From *KidScreen* magazine, quoted in *Children's Ministry*, July/August 2003, 3.

4. Strauss, William and Neal Howe, *Millennials Rising*, Vintage, 2000.

5. Doris Kearns Goodwin interview, Don Imus Radio Show, 2003.

6. Tapscott, Don, *Growing Up Digital: The Rise of the Net Generation*, McGraw-Hill, 1999. Quoted by Richard Tiplady, *Global Connections*, June 2000.

7. Richard Tiplady, *Global Connections* newsletter, June 2000.

8. Barna, George, *Generation Next*, Regal Books, 1995, 18-21.

two

The Beginning of Faith

Children are different from adults. Because they are in the process of growing and developing, they understand the world differently than adults do and relate to the world differently as well. But because it's difficult for adults to remember what it was like to think and feel as children, adults often fall into the trap of treating children as if they are just short adults and assuming they understand things they don't.

Our culture supports this fallacy by treating children like adults. We dress our children in adult clothes, and we expose them to situations and entertainment that were once considered to be for "adults only." All this is to say that when we talk about facilitating the spiritual formation of children, we need to remember that through the various stages of childhood children relate to God and understand God in ways that are different from those of adults. In addition, as they proceed through the developmental stages of life, they typically perceive spirituality in different ways at different stages. That means we must also understand something of the way children develop spiritually. We need to get into the minds, emotions, and spirits of children at various ages and stages to understand who they are and how God relates to them as preschool or grade school-age children. And even though worldviews, values, and priorities may change from generation to generation, most basic human developmental processes stay the same.

As parents and spiritual teachers of children, we need to understand that spiritual development is related to and intertwined with all the other types of development through which a child progresses. A child's emotional growth will greatly influence a child's affective understanding of God. And a child's spiritual growth, or lack thereof, can enhance or diminish her moral development. A child's growing intellectual abilities and analytical skills will directly impact how she understands faith concepts and learns to think with her soul. And a growing experiential understanding of faith concepts will help a child develop positive social skills and understandings.

So as we proceed with our discussion of ministry to and with children in 21st-century faith communities, we need to talk about child development and its symbiosis with spiritual development. In doing this I will refer to two social scientists, Erik Erikson and James Fowler, whose work, respectively, in the areas of psychosocial development and faith development are pertinent to our discussion.

Erik Erikson's theory of psychosocial development states that all human beings pass through eight stages or crises during their life spans. They begin in infancy and end as we face death. Erikson theorizes that the way in which a child or adult navigates each stage, either positively or negatively, will come to bear on the negotiation of the next stage and ultimately on the healthy or unhealthy emotional development of the person. For example, the very first of Erikson's stages is Trust vs. Mistrust. A positive navigation of this crisis will have the infant moving out of the stage with the ability to trust others and the world rather than a great mistrust of others. A positive outcome of this stage will enable the child to move into the second crisis of childhood, Autonomy vs. Shame/Doubt, ready to conquer it. A negative response to the first stage will hamper the child's navigation of the second stage and so on through all the stages.[1]

There are a number of factors that can push the child or adult into the next crisis; physical growth, intellectual development, and outside societal forces all move a person into the next stage. While the stages may be revisited, most people move through all eight stages during the course of life without getting stuck.

James Fowler is a social scientist well known for his research and extensive writing in the area of human faith development. While Fowler writes out of a personal Christian orientation, his work is broader than simply the development of the Christian faith—Fowler is interested in how human beings develop faith in any spiritual framework. Through extensive interviews about personal faith experience with many different types of people, Fowler developed six stages of faith formation beginning with infancy and proceeding through adulthood. Much of this process is dependent on the type of faith community the person belongs to and the inner desire of the person to move beyond his current stage of faith development. But it is important to note that, unlike in Erikson's model, a person can get stuck in any stage of the faith development process. While some organic developmental growth is necessary to push a person—a child in particular—to the next stage of growth, there is nothing to guarantee that any person will move on to the next stage.[2]

I believe the spiritual formation of the child begins at birth, at the very earliest (see Psalm 139). It may be positive or negative, but it is never neutral. In fact, Fowler believes infancy is a crucial foundational stage for all later positive faith development. Naturally, an infant has no concept of a world larger than himself and certainly no concept of any kind of God or faith. Yet the way the infant is cared for during those early months of life has direct bearing on his ability to form a relationship with God and with others in the faith community to which he belongs.

Erikson's work helps us understand the importance of these early moments of life as they relate to spiritual development. As I mentioned, Erikson's first stage is Trust vs. Mistrust. The child develops more trust than mistrust when the child has trustworthy, consistent caregivers and lives in a trustworthy, consistent environment. This means that if the child is fed when hungry, changed when wet and dirty, held when afraid or desiring of human contact, the child will be more likely to trust people than not. This primal and visceral sense of the safety of her environment gives an infant a sense that the world is a trustworthy place. But if these things are not present in the infant's environment, then the ability to have trusting, loving relationships with others can be severely disabled. The importance of trust in human development cannot be understated; our belief that other people will be good to us has to outweigh our belief that they will hurt us if we are to form loving attachments to other people.

It follows that the ability to trust others has direct bearing on our ability to have a relationship with God. If we cannot trust other people whom we can see and touch, how can we possibly hope to trust a God who is invisible and "out there" somewhere. But if we see others and the world at large as being more trustworthy than untrustworthy, we will find it easier to enter into a trusting relationship with God.

The Foundation of Faith

The early months of life are truly crucial to the positive spiritual formation and growth of all children. This understanding has obvious ramifications for parents. Clearly, parents can never go too far in their efforts to be trustworthy caregivers and to create a home that feels safe and loving. But this is also important information for those of us who care for children in our churches.

Often the work that happens in the church nursery is seen as little more than baby-sitting. No wonder it's hard to find committed volunteers! The caregivers in our church nurseries need to know that they are doing much more than helping parents. They need to understand that by loving, holding, feeding, and changing these babies, they are putting bricks in the foundation of trust these children will need in order to know and love God. Even the simple act of establishing and following safety guidelines in the nursery helps children understand that God's community of people is a safe and good place for them to be. Creating spaces where little fingers are safe from being stepped on or where tender bottoms fall on soft carpets will give the child a sense of being well cared for and safe. That coupled with consistent, loving caregivers who sing songs about Jesus or who tell the young child how God made her toes will build a foundation of trust the young child can transfer to the person of God.

Thinking of infants as spiritual beings also forces us to reconsider some of the ways we teach parents to care for

their children. Over the last 10 to 15 years many churches
have promoted a program designed to rigidly monitor an
infant's feeding and sleeping patterns. The theory is that
following this plan will develop an obedient and compliant
child, one who is ultimately obedient to God. But in reality
this kind of program requires parents to ignore the basic
needs of their babies—not feeding them during the night,
for example. But think about what a baby learns about
trust and mistrust when she cries from hunger or a wet
diaper and no one addresses her need. Following a protocol
like this with infants may very well form a child who will
obey the rules, but it will not form a child who will fall in
love with God.

The Independent Years

As children grow out of infancy and into the toddler years,
they begin to eagerly explore the world. This innate curiosity joins with their burgeoning physical and intellectual
abilities to push them into the next of Erikson's stages or
crises, Autonomy vs. Shame and Doubt. As he grows
increasingly independent of his parents, the toddler's battle
cries become, "Me do it" and "No." For a child to successfully navigate this crisis, he must come to feel good about
his newfound ability to master tasks like getting dressed,
using the toilet, and feeding himself rather than feel
ashamed or unsure of his ability to learn and execute new
and necessary skills. Adults who praise and celebrate the
child's age-appropriate attempts at independence help him
build a sense of competency. The parent or caregiver who
stifles or belittles a toddler's attempts at independence will
cast the pall of shame and doubt over the child's efforts at
conquering his little piece of the world.

Because a toddler's desire for independence often runs
headlong into his parents' desire to keep him safe, healthy,

and dressed, these are the years when discipline becomes
an issue. The way a child is disciplined has a tremendous
impact on this crisis of autonomy. The parent or caregiver
who expects behavior beyond the child's developmental
ability or offers harsh punishment for misbehavior can
damage the child's spirit and cause the child to lose confidence. The parent or caregiver who sets appropriate and
consistent expectations for a child's behavior and who follows up with appropriate, loving, and consistent consequences helps a child develop a sense of accomplishment.
A child who successfully negotiates this stage develops a
healthy self-concept that helps her see herself as lovable
and competent. Once I heard a story (which I hope is fictional) about a young seminary student who was assigned
as part of his field education experience to teach a class of
two-year-olds. The young man determined that the best
way to teach them was to sit the children on little chairs in
a row. He asked them to sit still while he pontificated on
the day's Bible story. Well, anyone who has had any experience with two-year-olds knows what happened next.
None of them stayed on their chairs for very long. To rem-
edy this situation the young seminarian blew a whistle
every time a child left his chair as a signal for the child to
sit back down. It's my best guess that there was a lot of
whistle blowing going on. While this story is amusing and
somewhat incredulous, it does make a point about age-
appropriate expectations and their importance to the development of a positive self-concept in children. Those two-
year-olds didn't know they didn't have the physical ability
to sit on a chair and listen for an extended period of time.
They also saw the adult who was telling them they should
do this as all knowing. Therefore, in their minds the adult
couldn't be wrong—so something was wrong with them if
they couldn't do what the adult asked. They would begin to
question their own competence. And because the teacher

inflicted a consequence (whistle blowing) every time a child left the chair, they knew they were making this all-important adult unhappy. So this experience left them questioning their ability to be loved as well.

This developing sense of self has a tremendous influence on a child's faith formation. Christians believe in a God who is pure love, a God who loved humans so much that when the ultimate sacrifice needed to be made, God was willing to die for us. The basis of forming a relationship with God is the acceptance of God's love for his human creations. If a child has been taught from his earliest years that he is not lovable or competent, not worth anything to anybody or to the world at large, that child is never going to truly believe God loves him. Forming that passionate love relationship God so desires from us will be difficult for the child who has never felt affirmation and love from the most important humans in her life. A child whose self-concept says, "I am lovable and competent" will be able to assert with confidence, "And God loves me, too." A child who is unsure of his ability to be loved and his ability to navigate the tasks of his life will have a more difficult time accepting God's boundless love.

Young children need to sense that they are lovable and competent from the important people in their lives not only because of the message it imprints on their sensitive psyches, but also because these people are the only concrete representations of God and Jesus they know. At this age a child's concept of God is vague and unformed. Young children live in a concrete world, and any concept as abstract as an invisible God is too much to understand.

But part of the work of early childhood is to make sense of this strange and fascinating world, so young children do their best to figure it out. One of the ways they understand God and Jesus is by giving godlike qualities to the people who have the most control over their lives—parents, preschool teachers, ministers, and religious education volunteers. To a young child each of these people seems all-powerful and all knowing. They have yet to discover that adults can't do everything and don't know everything. So if an adult tells a young child a story and says it's true, then in the child's mind it must be true because adults know everything. If a parent tells a child to behave in a certain way, the child believes she should be able to behave that way because Mom has told her she can, and Mom is never wrong. And if the people who tell the young child about Jesus and God act in loving and age-appropriate ways, the child understands that Jesus and God must be loving beings, too. Those of us involved in the spiritual nurture and formation of young children must always remember that we model God to these young minds and spirits in everything we do with them.

Preschoolers

As a child moves into the later preschool years, her faith goes through a stage James Fowler describes as Intuitive-Projective. The preschool child lives in a world of unrestrained imagination. She has very little concept of the logic of things and the world around her. These two aspects of the child's intellectual and affective development greatly influence her spiritual development. The stories, symbols, and gestures of faith form long-lasting emotional impressions that can have an almost indelible imprint on the child's later understanding of faith, God, and spirituality. Exposing children to the history and rhythms of the church year, the rituals of worship and community, and the stories of God's redemptive work in the world and God's specific work in our lives builds a foundation for positive faith development. However, images of a tyrannical, angry

God who inspires fear, Bible stories used as bludgeons to promote moralistic legalism, and visions of eternity spent writhing in hell will have lifelong negative implications for a child's faith.

The magnificent and untainted imagination of young children draws them toward the stories of the Bible. They are easily persuaded to wonder about the power, love, and mysteries of God. And they believe everything we tell them. So those of us entrusted with the soul care of young children need to work at introducing them to their loving Creator God. We need to acquaint them with God through ritual, story, community, and church tradition, helping them understand all this in a concrete and literal way.

For Erikson the preschool child is negotiating the psychosocial stage of Initiative vs. Guilt. The child has mastered the basic skills of life. She can feed herself, dress herself, and clean herself (to a certain extent). She can hold a conversation with another child or an adult. She can use scissors and crayons and markers to create crude representations of inanimate objects or people. Toward the end of this stage many children know their letters and can begin to read simple words. The world of school and the latent period of childhood are looming just around the bend. The child is poised for new and more complicated adventures.

And that is the crux of the crisis of this stage. The child at this stage will explore everything, ask questions about everything, and push every boundary that is set for her. The ways in which the adults in the child's life react to all that exploring, asking, and pushing will determine the positive or negative navigation of this stage.

A child who is discouraged, laughed at, or punished for taking reasonable risks or asking silly or outrageous (at least to the adult mind) questions will develop a strong sense of guilt that will follow her the rest of her life, causing her to put the brakes on risk-taking and creative thinking. But a child who is encouraged to explore within reasonable limits, a child whose questions are taken seriously and answered thoughtfully, who is presented with flexible-yet-safe, caring boundaries will grow up with a greater sense of competence and mastery of life. She will understand that it's okay to fail and okay to be disappointed some of the time. She will understand which things she should feel truly guilty about and which things get in the way of living life the way God desires us to live it. The child who leaves this stage with a sense of personal initiative will be a child who can love God with her whole heart, mind, and soul.

I have some friends who have two adult daughters who were parented extremely well. These girls are accomplished professionally, and both continue to pursue faith in God. I think one of the reasons for this is that each of these girls was allowed to explore ideas and diverse interests from the time they were young children all the way through young adulthood. Their parents were patient and hardy and had a good sense of humor as they followed these kids through cat shows and answered questions that would make even a good parent want to run screaming from the room. But all of this was done within the loving boundaries of this family's faith and social and relationship values. Fruit of this parenting continues to grow in the lives of these two remarkable young women.

At this stage in particular, a child's faith development is tightly tied to his intellectual development. So anytime we talk about the soul care of the young child, we need to talk about how his mind works. We need to talk about his intellectual development and the way he works to make sense of his world. The preschool child thinks very differently and understands the world around him very differently than does an adult. This makes for lots of problems when adults try to teach young children concepts of faith and the story of God.

Young children think concretely and literally. They cannot understand an abstract concept unless it is continually and intentionally linked with a concrete action or object. This is the reason adults find Bible-related object lessons so enjoyable and most young children don't get them at all. So say, for example, you are teaching a group of preschoolers that Jesus says we should love each other. If all you do is say to the children, "Jesus says we should love each other," they will sit there and smile at you and nod in agreement because you know everything and, of course, they know by now that they need to agree with anything Jesus said. And you may think you've communicated successfully that Jesus told us to love others.

Truth be told they have no idea what you are talking about because "love" or "loving others" is an abstract concept. In order to enable young children to understand abstract concepts, parents and teachers need to link them to something concrete and do it every time the action happens or the concept is discussed. I like to think of this as opening up little abstract-concept files in the child's brain where all the concrete actions are stored in the file one by one until the child reaches an age when the brain is able to process abstraction. Then all these bits and pieces in the file coalesce into the abstract concept. So when a child says something kind to another person, the caregiver or parent can say, "Those kind words showed love to Jennifer," and the concrete action of saying something kind will go into the "loving others" file. Or when the teacher or parent says that making a birthday card for an older person in the church is showing love to that person, then "making a birthday card" goes into the "loving others" file. Each time a concrete action is linked to an abstract concept the child is closer to understanding the larger idea.

Good and proper soul care during the earliest years of a child's life is the basis for a positive spiritual journey in later years. While young children won't understand God and the faith community in an intellectual way, they are capable of forming lasting attitudes about God, Jesus, and the importance of the community. If the child feels the faith community is a safe and loving place, then the child will have positive attitudes about being part of that community. If the child's parents and caregivers show that listening to and following God's story is a priority for them, then the child will model those attitudes. If the important adults in the child's life practice the spiritual disciplines, worship God, and make time to care for their own souls, then the child will find ways to mirror these behaviors in her own life. For the young child, spiritual understandings and practices are more caught than taught.

The positive spiritual formation of the young child was summed up concisely in a book published back in the 1980s written by Judith Shelly. She notes:

> Children have a natural interest in God and an inborn sense of the divine, the numinous, which must be nurtured by the family and community. Parents and other adult caretakers will help to determine if the future spiritual growth and development will be healthy or unhealthy by their actions and attitudes during those formative years. Three basic ingredients lay a healthy foundation for spiritual development: Unconditional love with plenty of positive reinforcement, realistic discipline which holds the child responsible for their actions within the limits of their abilities, and the support system which is dependable and truthful.[3]

The quality of the spiritual life of the preschool child will be directly proportional to the quality of the spiritual life of the child's parents and caregivers.

Notes

1. These theories of Erik Erikson found in *Childhood and Society* (second edition), W.W. Norton and Co., 1963.

2. These theories of James Fowler found in *Stages of Faith,* Harper and Row, 1981.

3. Shelly, Judith, *The Spiritual Needs of Children,* InterVarsity Press, 192, 34.

three

Bringing Faith to Life

As children move out of early childhood and into the elementary and adolescent years, their ability to trust others, to see themselves as capable and lovable, and their sense of initiative will propel them into new stages of emotional, physical, social, and spiritual development. Because older children are more verbal, more emotionally aware, and more likely to ask questions about what they don't understand, it's tempting to assume that their faith formation is quite straightforward. We teach them something, they take it in and seek clarification as needed, and the transfer of information is complete. Yet a closer look at both Erikson's stages of psychosocial development and Fowler's understanding of faith development makes it clear that there is much more happening in the hearts and minds of these children than meets the eye.

The elementary years of childhood are a time of learning and cementing the skills necessary to survive and be successful in life. Erikson says that children ages six to 12 are going through the crisis or stage of Industry vs. Inferiority. Because this is a time of intense learning, school-age children are very busy developmentally. To successfully navigate the elementary years the child must discover what she can do well and develop some basic competency in those necessary skills she cannot do well. The child who does this will see herself as industrious. On the other hand, the child who has difficulty in school and is unable to master basic life skills will emerge from this stage with a sense of inferiority that can weave its way into the rest of her life.

Unfortunately our society has upped the ante on the meaning of the words *necessary* and *competency*. There is great pressure on today's children to be successful in ways that are defined by outside influences—societal expectations, the media, even other children—not in ways defined by their own interests and abilities. Children are pushed to succeed academically, athletically, and socially in hopes that this will keep them in the game for admission to the best colleges and, ultimately, the best (read: most well-paying and prestigious) jobs. Today Erikson's concept of industry is defined in ways the late social scientist could have never imagined. Consequently, more children may be exiting this stage feeling more inferior than need be.

Certainly none of this frenetic pushing of children to be successful at all things has anything to do with the care of the child's soul, other than perhaps damaging it. This summer I realized that one of the positive aspects of the children's programs at my church was their noncompetitiveness. A remark made by one of my Vacation Bible School volunteers caused me to reflect on the idea that Vacation Bible School was perhaps the only summer activity these kids participated in that didn't ask them to compete with others or succeed at something. They could come to the church building each day and simply be children basking in the care of their small group leaders while eating cupcakes and building foam fish that flew like rockets.

Those of us who care for the souls of children in the church may need to think about how what we do helps children be children. We need to provide them respite from the daily push to be the best, which they face in every other arena of their lives. Helping a school-age child to love God has nothing to do with besting others in a competition, winning first prize at the science fair, or getting into an Ivy League school. But it has everything to do with helping the child understand that God loves him whether or not he can kick a soccer ball. God loves him whether or not he can conjugate French verbs. And God loves him even if he has to attend summer school to make up a failing grade. There are no inferior children as far as God is concerned.

Spiritually forming children means we help them see that in the economy of the kingdom of God being successful is loving others, showing mercy, fighting for justice, and walking humbly with God. And this is not an easy task. I work every day with what I call "children of privilege." These children are good kids. There's not really a discipline problem among them. They're bright and fun and winsome. But they can't imagine a world without the things they have. They can't imagine a world where they don't go to a cabin on the lake in the summer or a Caribbean vacation in the winter. What I want them to know and to practice is not that it is wrong or sinful to go on a Caribbean vacation but that because they have that privilege, they also have great responsibility to use that privilege to further the kingdom of God on earth. I've not yet figured out all the answers about how to teach this, but some ideas laid out in later chapters may be helpful.

The ways in which the school-age child understands faith and the faith community is tied inherently to the child's intellectual development. During the school years a child's thinking and reasoning ability move from the fanciful and illogical thinking of the preschool child to what is called concrete, operational thinking. While they still cannot necessarily reason abstractly, they are beginning to understand and order their worlds in a logical fashion. Cause and effect, space, and time begin to make sense to them. If you tell a school-age child that an event will last an hour, she can intellectually approximate how much time that is. She can figure out simply by looking if certain objects will fit inside certain kinds of containers. The preschool child can do neither of these things.

For this reason school-age children do much better with understanding the cultural milieu of the Bible than do preschool children. They can begin to understand how long ago 8,000 or 2,000 years was. They realize that different cultures around the world live in different ways, and this helps them understand that the culture and way of life of the people in Bible times was very different from the life they lead. This concrete reasoning ability also helps children to begin understanding how other people feel about things. Preschoolers have no idea that other people feel pain the way they do because they are in the egocentric stage of development, but school-age children begin to have the ability to empathize.

This shift in the way a child processes and understands her world also impacts her faith. Fowler describes this stage of faith formation as the Mythic-Literal stage. The symbol, ritual, and story of the child's faith community are integrated into the child's personality, and the child takes these on as her own. This does not mean the child has critically evaluated the beliefs of the community and chosen them because they make sense. The school-age child does not have the reasoning abilities to do this. Instead because the child is immersed in the community, she simply wraps herself in what she knows best. She emulates the people she knows best—her parents and those in the community who know her and care for her. She begins to identify with the place that provides her with comfort, safety, friends, and belonging.

For example, children at this age have moved away from the self-centered mentality of preschoolers who have little concept of the needs and feelings of others. The elementary child is learning to negotiate social situations, to take others into consideration. He identifies with people like him and recognizes that there are people who behave differently than he does. This budding sense that the world consists of different people with different abilities and desires gives him a strong belief in a God with human characteristics. It makes sense that God is loving, kind, and caring because he knows that's how people should treat each other. He understands that God can feel joy and pain, just like he can. He begins to recognize that God isn't just an imaginary being but someone he can know and trust.

Elementary children also have a strong need for justice. They hold to the naïve premise that goodness should and will always be rewarded and that evil should and will always be punished. They order their understanding of the world and of God on this premise.

This understanding accounts for elementary children's inherent need to have everything in their lives be fair. Anyone who has ever led a competitive game with school-age children knows how alert they are for any infraction by the other team or any subtle change in the rules that may give the competitor an edge. Any parent who has split a cookie between two children knows that it's the eight-year-old who will complain about unequal portions, not the three-year-old. The world of the elementary child is black and white with no room for gray areas.

This concrete understanding of right and wrong makes school-age children exceptionally open to the faith modeling of the adults in their lives. This is the stage where children make active choices between right and wrong. They are now able to understand that there are acceptable ways to treat people, to make decisions, to live in communities. They get that there are rules and expectations. As caregivers, then, we need to pay particular attention to the desire these children have to do what's right. We need to show them what it means to live with integrity even when life doesn't seem fair. We need to explain to them why we act with kindness even when others are unkind. These are the years when a child's sense of morality kicks into gear. If we miss the opportunity to help children figure out how to choose good when the stakes are relatively low, we will have a tremendous challenge on our hands as the elementary years turn into the teen years and the stakes become much, much higher.

Preteen Trauma

As we get older, the rate at which we move through the stages of development slows down considerably. As that relates to children, the crisis of Industry vs. Inferiority doesn't end with the move to middle school. In fact, in many ways the crisis becomes more urgent for the child. As preteens become more independent and maneuver through the complex social structures of middle school, a large number of them shift from a sense of industry to a sense of inferiority and back again.

Developmentally, the preteen years mark the move from concrete operational reasoning abilities to abstract reasoning. Preteens gradually realize that life is indeed unfair, that good people can make bad choices, and that some of those choices have mild consequences while others administer serious blows. At the same time, the physical and emotional changes preteens experience create an unprecedented level of confusion and stress in their lives. Their bodies change, their friendships change, their social settings change. Nearly every element of a preteen's life will go through some kind of alteration during the ages of 10 to14—some of which they will welcome, others of which they will curse.

As a preteen enters this stage where everything is up for grabs, his faith will go through a major shift of its own. The preteen years mark the beginning of the challenge to childhood faith that will continue during the teen and young adult years. Preteens need to have this challenge taken seriously. Parents and caregivers should not be afraid of this faith crisis; it is a natural part of human development and can ultimately result in the child having a stronger, more active, and more fulfilling faith in God. Preteens should never be told they are displeasing God by having these feelings and questions. Instead, every attempt should be made to answer these questions candidly and truthfully.

When I explore the Bible and faith concepts with preteens, I always ask them what questions they have about what we've just talked about or experienced. And I tell them no question is out of bounds. Then I do my best to answer as truthfully and accurately as I can the questions asked. Even when the questions border on silly (with this age group it's a given that someone will ask a question designed to inflame the rest of the group to silliness), I try to find a kernel of truth or seriousness in the question and answer that. Usually I've found they have a lot of questions and appreciate having these questions taken seriously.

Preteens are also on the lookout for role models who can show them what matters in life. They need to hear the stories of those who live their faith holistically, who take the call of God on their lives seriously. Whether it's

Grandpa talking about the ways his faith sustained him during the war or the story of a missionary who sacrificed everything to share God's love, preteens are looking for adults who live their faith with integrity. This ties into Fowler's assessment of the Mythic-Literal stage of faith formation. During the preteen years, children will decide if they are going to buy into the faith of their family and community or if they will instead forge a new path for themselves. The modeling they see in us will play an enormous part in their decision.

Evangelizing Children

The school-age years are the time that many churches and parachurch organizations advocate the aggressive evangelization of children. That long-cited statistic that most people of faith come to faith prior to the age of 14 and the conservative, evangelical church's emphasis on a crisis-conversion experience have led to an array of products and curricula meant to help churches save children. Whole educational programs are designed around the goal of getting children to "pray the prayer" and cross over the line from "lost" to "saved."

Unfortunately, once the prayer is prayed, parents and religious education leaders often breathe a sigh of relief. "Whew! That one's taken care of." I have a friend who is the children's pastor at a large midwestern church. Each week he has to give a report to the senior pastor citing how many children were "saved" in his programs. This number is a measure of the effectiveness of his children's programming. But parents and churches who are truly interested in the positive soul care of the child will not be as concerned about this one-time experience as they will about the ongoing immersion of the child in the things of God and Jesus.

Horace Bushnell was a 19th-century New England pastor concerned about the spiritual formation of children. His ministry coincided with one of the New England revivals and he was deeply troubled by the revivalists' attempts at bringing children to faith. Evangelists were treating children as miniature adults, passing on to impressionable children the same message of hellfire and damnation. Bushnell felt that scaring children into the kingdom of God was counterproductive. He believed that children from faithful Christian homes did not need the crisis-conversion experience advocated by the revivalists.

His book *Christian Nurture* is an attempt to lay out his understanding of how children come to know and love God. Bushnell states, "My argument is to establish that the child is to grow up a Christian and never know himself as being otherwise."[1] Bushnell thought the children of Christian parents should be so immersed in a Christian environment both at home and at church, that they would never think of themselves as anything but Christian. They would always love God. They would always follow Jesus. They would grow up to be people of faith.

God has given children an innate ability to know and love God. Children are strongly attracted to God from birth. This is the quality that needs to be nurtured from birth onward, both at home and in the faith community. Our children need to be told they are Christians and treated as such—invited into the rituals and rites of the church, treated as full members of the community, given opportunities to lead in the community, and loved as Jesus calls us to love each other as a sign of God's love for the world.

This is how children come to love God and follow Jesus. Waiting for a child to pray a prayer before that child is seen as worthy of community participation wastes valuable faith-nurturing time. Scaring children into God's arms with stories of sin and hell only skews their view of God and teaches them things they need to unlearn later in life in order to have a passionate love relationship with God. Asking children to come forward or raise a hand in response to an evangelistic message only goads children into responding for the wrong reasons, such as pleasing a parent or teacher, following the crowd, or gaining a prize.

Now this is not to say that there won't ever come a time in a child's life where the child says to God, "I love you, and I want to follow Jesus." My own childhood conversion experience is something like that. I grew up in a church where I heard a lot about accepting Jesus as my Savior. I heard about going to hell if I didn't do this. I knew this was something my parents and my Sunday school teachers wanted me to do. But even as a seven-year-old I didn't want to do it for the wrong reasons.

It was summer, and my church friends had gone to a Christian camp in New Hampshire. During that week several of them had accepted Jesus as their Savior. They'd prayed the prayer. They were in. I heard about this and remember thinking that this was perhaps something I should do. So all week I pondered my need to accept Jesus. I wanted to make sure I wasn't doing it just because my friends had. Finally I decided it was something I wanted to do and that I wasn't just jumping on the Jesus bandwagon. That Sunday morning all by myself in my bedroom I officially accepted Jesus. But as I look at the steps leading to that moment, I think my actions had more to do with the nurture of my family and the people who cared about me at church than all the little evangelistic talks I'd heard.

Was I a Christian before I prayed the prayer? I think so. Was I a better Christian after I prayed the prayer? Not necessarily. There wasn't much in my seven-year-old life that needed to change. Perhaps praying the prayer helped give some definition and accountability to what I believed. It certainly raised my profile at my small fundamentalist church (my mother, of course, had to tell everyone what I'd done). But I don't really think I moved from one cosmic state to another.

Interestingly, of those church friends who prayed the prayer at camp that summer, none of them are following Jesus today. So will they be part of God's new kingdom because they prayed the prayer 40 years ago? I don't know.

I believe the time has come for churches to reconsider the overt evangelizing of children. The approaches typically used have little to no bearing on what's actually happening in a child's heart and mind. For the most part these tactics are manipulative, playing on the child's emotions and desire to be accepted and loved. A faith community should never be involved in manipulating the soul of a child.

The Process of Faith

Lawrence Richards is a longtime observer and critic of the way churches typically teach children about faith. He feels that most churches are more interested in the cognitive schooling of children about faith than in actually nurturing them and caring for their souls. In several of his books, he outlines five processes for guiding the spiritual development of children in the faith community.[2] I think these tenets can be helpful for nurturing children in the emerging church.

First, Richards says that children need to be involved in processes that communicate belonging. An affective relationship with people in the faith community other than their parents and relatives is an important piece of their spiritual nurture. Children must feel they belong in their faith community as much as the adults do. It's not enough to say, "Children are welcome here." This belonging needs to be demonstrated through the policies and practices of the community. Forming relationships with children is the responsibility of all members of the community, not just those who work with them in educational programs.

Second, Richards says children need to be guided in processes that involve participation. For positive spiritual nurture to happen, children must be allowed to participate in the activities and rituals of the faith community. They cannot be shunted off to the basement of the church building while the adults do the real business of faith. The child needs to do things in the community, not just have things done for her. The faith community should intentionally provide opportunities for the child to act on her faith, such as expressing it in worshiping God or serving others. In addition, children need to experience the stories of faith, not just hear them. Childhood religious education needs to be experiential. Children should be provided with opportunities to play with the stories of the Bible through tactile materials, imaginative play, and physical activity. They should have time to explore the reasons why each story is an important part of the story of their faith.

The third process of spiritual development is the modeling of adult lives in front of the children. When the child brushes up against people of faith through this participation in the life of the community, the child sees models of faith. The child sees adults who struggle, who trust God, who make mistakes and are forgiven, who work for mercy and justice, who model kingdom values. This modeling is powerful teaching for children—more powerful for faith development than listening to a hundred Bible stories or watching a month's worth of VeggieTales videos. Children will remember the people of the faith community and their lives more than any Bible facts they learned at a church program.

Richards' fourth process is for children to be guided in instructional processes as interpretations of life. Churches are far too dependent on the formal schooling model for instruction about faith. If we know anything at all about children, it's that they tend to learn more through informal and nonformal means of education than through sitting in a classroom. The lessons learned through writing and art projects, opportunities for service, and even simple walks outside will stick with children long after they've forgotten how many sons Noah had.

Richards' fifth process of spiritual development for children is to help and encourage them in the exercise of choice making. From their earliest years our children need to be taught how to make good choices. After all, following Jesus is about making good and appropriate choices. Every day each of us is confronted with the choice to follow Jesus through the options presented to us or to go another way. Understanding how to evaluate these options and think through the possible consequences, good and bad, is an important life and soul skill for children to develop.

We can start teaching children how to make good choices in their early years. Young children can be given the opportunity to make clothing and food choices. Offering a preschooler the choice between a jelly sandwich and a tuna fish sandwich may not seem like a big deal, but it helps the child develop choosing skills. If the child is not happy with the choice, it helps him understand what it means to live with the consequences of a choice and perhaps enables him to choose more carefully the next time. Practicing choice making is the only way children will learn to make good and good pleasing choices.

Children can also be challenged to make choices to live intentionally in God's way and see what happens. Debriefing the child on the results of these choices can help him see and experience that following God's way is the better choice. If we never allow children to think about their choices, we limit their ability to make good decisions. At the same time we can't just leave children to their own devices with the hope that they'll learn from their mistakes. As caregivers we need to offer children choices within the boundaries of appropriate and safe behavior. A friend of mine who works with young teenagers likens this balance to building a strong, sturdy fence to keep the child safe and then giving him unlimited freedom to explore the confines of that space.

God surrounded children with adults both in the extended biological family and the community of faith for a reason. Parents and other adults are there to guide, teach, and model life for our children. Not only are we to teach things like how to button a button, use a spoon, and throw a baseball, but we are also to pass on the things of God and Jesus through our relationships with these children. No church program, camp, video series, or Sunday school curriculum can emulate the power these relationships have in the spiritual formation of children. No child can truly come to know God without the influence of caring, godly adults in her life. The soul care of children is an awesome responsibility, one every parent and participant in a community of faith needs to take seriously.

God intended for children to go through certain developmental processes. God understands how preschoolers order their worlds better than any developmental psychologist ever could. God understands how a grade school-age child thinks about Bible stories and how a child comes to faith. God is the author of all of this. God wants us to care for children in ways that will enhance their spiritual development at each age. God wants us to be faithful in the soul care of our children, and God will take care of the rest.

Notes

1. Bushnell, Horace, *Christian Nurture,* Baker, 1979 (reprinted from the 1861 edition), 10.

2. Larry Richards' five processes of spiritual development can be found in *Theology of Children's Ministry,* Zondervan, 1983, 76.

four

The Role of Community

One of my favorite weekly times at my church is in between our two worship services when everyone bumps into each other in the hallway and greets and chats. Children race in between the adult conversations or shyly hide behind an extroverted parent. All the generations socialize together without even thinking about it. No one planned or programmed this time. To me this is the time when my church looks most like a biblical community. But even without a coffee-time minister in charge of making this informal social time happen, it took some maneuvering to create intergenerational fellowship.

A little over a year ago there were two distinct gatherings between the services. Coffee was served outside the Meeting House, far away from where the children and youth had their educational programs. Older adults and empty nesters primarily populated this coffee klatch—no racing children or gawky teenagers allowed. Around the corner and down the hall from this conclave was the bagel table. For a dollar and change one could partake of a bagel, cream cheese, milk, or juice. Children and teens swarmed around the bagel table each week while their parents talked with other parents. The demographic was birth through about 45 years old.

While both social times were vibrant and noisy, neither one reflected our full community. It seemed a simple thing to me that if we really intended to be the true community of faith, as we told people we were, then we ought not to have these two generationally separate social times on Sunday morning. The solution seemed simple. "Let's move the coffee to where the bagels are," I said frequently in our weekly staff meetings. The rest of the staff smiled benignly at me like I was that odd relative who shows up at family functions and throws off the delicate balance of the familial dynamics. Our senior minister told me the problem was that I was making much too much sense.

Then one day, with really no fanfare or discussion, the coffee showed up in the same place as the bagels. I still don't really know how it happened. Some of the older people were nonplussed as they left the worship service only to find a lack of coffee in its usual place. They needed to get used to the idea of making two left turns after leaving the worship service in order to find their cup of church coffee. Some were distressed that they would have to hang out with the noisy children, but they've either gotten used to this or gone to Starbucks for their Sunday morning caffeine fix. By now most have made the transition well, and the in-between service time has become a microcosm of the community we're trying to create, with all the generations together and enjoying themselves.

All churches are some kind of social community, but it takes thought, intent, and hard work to become a biblical community of faith that is foundational to the spiritual development not only of its children, but also of all its members. Most churches believe themselves to be these kinds of communities. But just because people come to your church does not mean you have a community conducive to spiritual formation. Just because people come to your church does not mean you have a community welcoming to all generations and people of diversity.

The Faith-Community Connection

I grew up in a small church on the Connecticut shoreline. I don't remember a lot about the teaching I received in that church. I don't remember most of the sermons or Sunday school lessons I sat through. But I do remember the people. I remember the older woman who was our children's choir director and who served us soda and doughnuts after each rehearsal. I remember Ruby, our pastor's mother, who was my Sunday school teacher for more years than I can count. I remember the adults who knew my name and knew who I was as a part of that church. And I remember the things the community did together and how the children were included. I remember church picnics and potluck dinners. And I remember how several of my friends and I were often allowed to sing in the evening services—impromptu special music that was probably hard on the ears of the congregation yet made us feel a part of the community.

I know that in some way growing up in and being embraced as an equal member of that faith community, a church that would never make anyone's list of the best churches in America, contributed to my spiritual growth and my continued determination to hold on to this faith of my childhood. Religious educator John Westerhoff writes, "If our children are to have faith, we need to make sure that the church becomes a significant community of faith."[1]

Faith is not something that develops in a vacuum. Having faith, understanding faith, exploring faith, and questioning faith are not solo activities. These things are meant to be done with others who are on the same path or looking for the same path. These things are meant to be done with people older than us, the same age as us, and younger than us. These things are meant to be done with people who look, think, and live differently than we do. In other words, faith only matures when it is exposed to the spiritual hothouse of a biblical covenant community. When our churches segregate children from the rest of the community, we stunt the spiritual formation of the entire community.

The Marks of Community

John Westerhoff defines community primarily as a group of people who share a common memory or tradition.[2] In other words, a community is a group of people who have shared life together and have stories of that life together.

Once I was on the pastoral staff of a megachurch. The senior pastor valued closeness in our staff relationships, and he believed that one of the ways we'd develop this was through shared experiences. So four times a year we went on retreats together. Some were planning retreats. Some were field trips to interesting places around our city. We toured a sports arena, visited the local county jail, and observed a surgery at a world-famous hospital. Other trips were to churches in the area to talk with their staffs about how they viewed and conducted themselves as churches. We were required to attend "game nights" at the senior pastor's home. The only reasons permissible for missing a staff meeting were being out of town or being deathly ill.

And it worked: the more of these experiences we shared, the closer we became as a staff. We came close to becoming a small community. Even now when I get together with these men, our talk often turns to those shared adventures. We became a community through our shared and remembered life together. If our children are to develop good memories of their early life in a faith community, they must have chances to share life with the faith community.

Second, Westerhoff says a community is a group of people who share common goals and purposes. It is a group of people who are working together toward a communal accomplishment. There is something about working on a project together or going through situations together in order to reach a goal that binds people together. There is something about sharing a purpose or wishing for the same situational outcome that causes groups to put aside differences, even delight in differences, in order to make the wished-for thing happen. But if a group is at cross-purposes or has opposing dreams for an organization, it will never be able to truly share life together. People will never be able to fully trust each other because of this disagreement over outcomes and goals. Authentic community cannot happen when there is dissention over the goals and purposes of the group.

The third characteristic of a community is a clear sense of group identity. Personal identity—a clear understanding of oneself as independent of others—is essential for healthy emotional growth. If we don't know who we are apart from our family, friends, or culture, then we will constantly try on new identities, and that will hinder our intimacy with others. This can happen with group identity as well. If a group does not have a clear picture of who they are and what that means for the actions and life of the group, then the group will be constantly trying on new identities, resulting in confusion for the group members and possible conflict between the group members.

Finally, Westerhoff says that a faith community conducive to the soul care of its members must consist of at least three generations. Because development of community depends on shared stories, traditions, and memories, there must be people in the community who can pass those memories and traditions on to those who are too new or too young to have experienced them. In the megachurch mentioned earlier, the older staff members often helped the newer staff assimilate by regaling them with stories of staff triumphs and gaffes from years past. A community must include people who can pass on the goals and purposes of the community and model the community's identity to the younger members.

At the same time, younger, newer members of the community are needed to create new traditions or new, more up-to-date understandings of the older ones. Younger members will reflect God's story and the story of the community back to the older members of the community in new and challenging ways. The presence of and communication between three or more generations in a faith community is essential for the spiritual development of that community and its members.

My community tries to program events that bring the generations together in hopes that as a result of being active together, children, adults, and teens will meet each other and begin to get to know each other and our stories. Each spring we hold an all-church retreat (a bit of a misnomer since only about 20 percent of the community makes the four-hour trip to the camp in northern Minnesota). But those who attend hail from all the generations represented in our community. We are intentional about providing little in the way of age-stratified programming during the retreat. Instead we try to create activities in which all the generations can participate. We play group games, do the Bunny Hop and the Hokey Pokey, and hold a talent night where anyone of any age and talent can participate. And they do, from a 96-year-old woman reciting poetry to a six-year-old Suzuki violinist.

On Shrove Tuesday, we hold a pancake supper to mark the beginning of the Lenten season. Everyone in the church community is invited to come, and we party together. We stuff ourselves with pancakes, have our faces painted, wear brightly colored Mardi Gras masks, blow bubbles, participate in pancake races, sing silly songs, and then wave good-bye to the "Alleluias" for the duration of Lent. We don't vary the program much from year to year because we want this to become a tradition, part of the shared memory and story of our community. We want children, teens, and adults to pass the lore of the Shrove Tuesday pancake dinner on to succeeding generations.

It's amazing to watch what happens at these community events. People of all ages meet each other, see each other, and talk to each other, perhaps for the first time. Older people care for other people's children—something they might never think of doing in a formal way on a Sunday morning. Children move comfortably in and out of the activities. And this carries over to other parts of community life. For the first few years we held the all-church retreat, we transported all the campers up north on large tour buses. One little girl whiled away the time on the bus by being entertained by several adults. She remembered these people from the bus trip and the retreat. From then on whenever she came to community activities on Sunday mornings, she had to find and greet all those people, or her church experience was not complete.

We often think of communities as groups of people with specific things in common—a zip code, a belief system, an income bracket. And yet exclusivity is never a characteristic of a biblical faith community. All are welcome to come and participate in the community, no matter what. Authentic Christian community demands that we forge relationships with people who are different from us (remember the Good Samaritan?). As our society becomes more and more economically, politically, and racially stratified, it has become even more important for faith communities to exemplify inclusiveness. A truly loving, all encompassing, and diverse faith community models the love of God for all to the rest of the world better than any exclusively anglocentric, evangelistic message ever can.

Positive faith communities are places where people care for each other, where no one person is independent of the others. Communities are places where all of life is shared on some level: the good, the bad, the messy, the shameful, the startling, and the fantastic. It should be the one place where those who are wounded, whether by others or by their own inappropriate choices, can come for balm and healing. The faith community needs to be a grace-filled place where God's love and forgiveness is modeled for all to see.

Notes

1. Westerhoff, John, *Will Our Children Have Faith?* Harper and Row, San Francisco, 1976, 54.

2. These characteristics of community are found in Chapter 3 of *Will Our Children Have Faith?*

five

Children in Community

Recently our preschool children sang a song
as part of a worship service devoted to highlighting the
lives of the children of our faith community. Many of these
children had been living in community with each other
each week as they heard God's story and worshiped God
together. They'd learned about what it meant to be in the
presence of God and what it meant to sing songs in praise
of God. Many of them were on the cusp of grasping that
singing during a worship service was more than a perform-
ance, more than entertaining the adults—it was about helping all the generations worship God.

However, there were a few children who, while con-
nected to our church, were not a regular part of this community experience, and one could tell the difference
through their actions and attitudes toward what they were
doing. There was an appreciable and notable difference

between the children whose faith and attitudes were being formed consistently by community values and those who had not had this experience. Our faith communities form our faith experience, form our actions and attitudes, whether we are intentional about it or not—so let's create faith communities that positively influence children to love God and follow Jesus.

But understanding what makes a community work is only part of the picture. In order to create communities in which our children can thrive, we also need to have a sense of why positive community life is so essential to their faith formation. Once we recognize how communities influence children, it becomes clear that there is truly no way to form children without community.

Belonging

After studying numerous faith communities, social scientist Steve Sandage identified five characteristics of community life that have particular influence on the spiritual care and formation of its members.

The first of these characteristics is belongingness, or the level of acceptance a person experiences in his faith community.[1] It makes sense that when a person feels an emotional connection to a group and feels safe enough in the group to tell the truth about himself, he is able to open himself up to God's work in his life. We often define belongingness simply in terms of feeling part of a social group. While this is indeed part of feeling accepted by a group, it is only a superficial understanding of real belonging. The real test of belongingness is a person's freedom to be honest, transparent, and authentic with others in the group without fear of reprisal or ostracism.

I was once part of a small group of women who were part of my larger church community. I was elated to be invited to participate in this group because I respected these women and hoped I would develop some solid friendships with them. I made a deliberate decision to trust these women and believe in what I thought to be their acceptance of me. I shared personal things with them and told the truth about who I was at that time in my life. At no time did any of these women tell me or show me they were not interested in supporting me in the difficulties I was going through.

What I didn't know is that they were viewing me as "needy" and "high maintenance," which perhaps I was at the time. So I kept sharing myself with them. Only later, after the group disbanded, did I discover that the group had really disbanded largely because they didn't want to deal with me. I felt betrayed and ashamed. If they had only stopped me at the beginning by telling me they didn't want me to talk about these things, I would have understood the parameters of these relationships. I thought I belonged, and I thought I was accepted. It was a shock to find out that wasn't true.

Faith communities need to assess how well they do on the belongingness scale and how accepting they want to be of others. But those communities that are accepting, show grace, and allow people to be their authentic selves will reap the benefits of being a community where true spiritual formation and soul care can happen.

A sense of belonging is of paramount importance to children. Children need to know that when they walk through the door of their church building, they are welcome and valued as much as the adults. The soul care of our children depends on their knowing that the church is their church. They need to know the names of the people they see when they walk through the door. And those adults need to know the names of the children.

The young daughter of our Minister of Music loves to come to church for the simple reason that when she walks down the hall, people call out her name and give her hugs. These are the people she looks forward to seeing each week. These people are an important part of her community and spiritual experience. Children need to be greeted by the greeters in the same way the adults are. They need opportunities to work alongside adults in the work of the church and to worship with adults. One of our ushers always has his young daughters beside him, helping him hand out the Sunday bulletin to arriving worshipers.

I had worked in one church for just a few months when I found myself in a Vacation Bible School planning meeting. We were discussing plans for the preschoolers' portion of Vacation Bible School and were talking about contingency plans for their game time in case of inclement weather. I suggested that if it rained, we could bring them upstairs to the large open common area outside the church's worship center. The other women at the meeting looked at me as if I'd just arrived from another planet. "We're not allowed to bring the children upstairs," one of them finally explained. I couldn't believe what I was hearing, and I assured them that if we needed to, we would bring the children upstairs. Fortunately I never had to test my resolve, but I continue to be mystified that any church would have places where children are not allowed. No place in a church building should be off limits to its children. After all, as a friend of mine used to say, it's a church, not a museum.

One of the grave errors churches make is to view children simply as consumers of church services rather than as valued members of the community. Our children need to be appreciated by the other generations for their unique contributions to the community and for their unique personalities and dispositions. They need space in the church building they can call their own, but they also need to know that they are welcome to the adult spaces of the church as well. When children know they belong, they will open themselves up not only to accept all the good things the community has to offer them, but also to share all the good things they have to offer.

Trust

Faith communities also help members develop what Sandage calls "moral trust." This pertains to the group's perception of the authority structure of the community. Does the rank and file of the community view the group's leadership as predictable? Or conversely, does the leadership seem scattered or perhaps capricious? Does the leadership allow for all voices to be heard or are all decisions made from the top down? How is power and authority viewed and used by the community's leaders? The answers to these questions contribute to the level of community trust in the leadership.

In order for a faith community to facilitate positive spiritual growth in its members, it must be seen as safe and trustworthy. Unsafe communities do not allow people to be authentic. Unsafe communities do not allow people to be vulnerable. Unsafe communities do not offer an environment where community members can explore their faith, question their faith, and think outside the box about their faith, all essential factors in spiritual growth. But morally trustworthy leadership and communities are places where faith and life can be explored without reprisal and without expectations of absolute certainty.

While our children may not understand the type of leadership or governance a faith community has, they will understand if the community is a safe and secure place for them. We can demonstrate the trustworthiness of our faith communities by creating an environment where young children feel cared for and safe from harm, where children's spaces are free from hazards, where they know someone will take care of them in an emergency. Children trust their environment when the expectations of their behavior are appropriate and within their abilities. They trust the adults around them when the boundaries and consequences are loving, clear, and consistent.

In the last 10 to 15 years, churches have become more and more aware of the need to know the backgrounds of the people they allow to volunteer in their children's programs. Overall this is a good thing. These background checks and security measures help the parents in your community feel that this is a safe place for their children, and these safeguards protect the vulnerable in your community from those who would choose to prey on them in evil and unspeakable ways. They help to make your community trustworthy.

But I think churches need to explore how these safeguards and procedures hinder the faith community from being what it truly needs to be in a biblical sense. Recently I was part of a three-day discussion with children's pastors from large churches all around the United States. One was sharing the screening and protective procedures they had in place. First, he explained, they had an armed off-duty police officer patrolling their church campus. Now this church isn't located in the inner city or a war zone; it's part of an affluent suburb in the middle of the United States of America. I'm just not sure that an armed guard ever belongs in the middle of a biblical community of faith and certainly not in one where there is no real threat of violence. The lessons of Jesus were about making the world a better place by ushering in the kingdom of God. Jesus told his disciples that the rest of the world would recognize them by the way they loved each other in their small community. Permitting an armed guard in your church community does not paint a picture of a group of people who trust each other or who trust and love God.

This children's pastor went on to describe how their Children's Ministry building is locked down each Sunday as a means of protecting their children. Parents and children are allowed into the building only if they can present their church-issued identity cards. If a family has been careless enough to leave this card at home, they must either go home and retrieve the card or not be allowed into the building. Now I'm all for protecting children, but at some point I believe congregations need to discuss seriously when these security procedures hinder the building of true community. We need to reconcile the real need for risk-management procedures with the real need to be biblical communities of faith that are welcoming to all. We need to have the courage to say, "Enough is enough! What we have in place now will adequately protect our children and still enable us to be the loving, trusting community God wants us to be."

Because positive biblical community is so integral to the healthy spiritual development of children, we want to be very careful that we balance the needs of the whole community with the need to protect the vulnerable members of the community. If we provide our children with so much protection that they are never able to experience the full and true community, then we have done them a disservice by denying them a piece of the kingdom of God.

Sharing Gifts

Belonging and trust pave the way for a third element of spiritual growth through community: mutual gifting. Communities exhibit this characteristic when members feel they are welcome and invited to share their gifts and resources with the rest of the body. This can include the sharing of spiritual gifts but also things like hospitality, generosity, healing, and personal talents. People who are allowed to contribute to the community tend to get the most out of the community and feel the most favorable toward the community. People who are allowed to use their gifts and talents to contribute to the well being of the community tend to be more committed to it than those who sit on the sidelines.

As people who work with children, we need to think about ways the gifts and talents of our children can be used in the life of the faith community. Earlier I mentioned how as a child I was allowed to sing with my friends during our Sunday evening services. And as a fledgling piano student I was also sometimes asked to play during our worship services. Now I wasn't very proficient at either of these things, but being allowed to and asked to share these pieces of myself with the greater faith community helped shape my sense of belonging and my connectedness to that small church. At my current church we invite children to act as lectors during our worship services one Sunday each month. During each of these Sunday morning worship services, children read the Scripture passages for the day— both leading and participating in worship.

The key to inviting children to use their gifts and talents in the service of the community is being intentional about identifying them and then asking the children to put those gifts to use for the good of the community. Too often we think of children's ministry as doing something for our children. We need to expand our thinking to see that it is also working with our children and allowing them to minister to the adults. But we need to take the time to think creatively about what it is our children can contribute and then find ways to make that contribution meaningful for them and for the other generations of the community.

At my church we've experimented with creating worship experiences meaningful to all generations (and you'll hear more about these in a later chapter). One element I've sought to include in every experience we've created is to have the children make something that will contribute to the worship of all who are in attendance at that service. So the Sunday prior to a worship experience that was to be centered on the story of Jesus' multiplication of the loaves and fishes, the children baked flat bread to use during the next week's visual depiction of the story. The week prior to preaching a sermon on Peter's attempt to walk on the water, the children and I painted large, poster-sized pictures of the events of the Bible story. Then the next Sunday, as I told the story as part of my sermon, I held up the pictures for the entire congregation to see. I had adults tell me they wished we used visual aids for the sermon every week.

My associate for preschool ministries has involved the children he works with in a ministry of encouragement to the leaders of the church. Several times a year the young children make and color cards that say, "We're praying for you." (And, of course, in their Sunday morning worship times they do pray for these leaders.) Then these cards are mailed to our deacons and church council members. I received an e-mail from one of our leaders, a businessman a long way removed from knowing any of our preschoolers, who said receiving that card was one of the most encouraging things that had ever happened to him in the many years he had been at this church.

Allowing children to serve the church with their gifts and talents cements them to the faith community and gives them a solid base of people who know and love them. This can reap enormous spiritual benefits when the children reach adolescence and young adulthood. These opportunities promote that feeling of belonging to the faith community so important for children's spiritual growth. And adults grow spiritually when they accept gifts from children and allow children to serve them. It is a reminder of what being a person of faith is all about.

Citizenship

This means community members sense that their church helps them find ways to contribute to the greater good of the larger extended community and to the rest of the world. Positive faith communities are not inward looking. Positive faith communities help their members to see that people of God have a larger responsibility to the world God created and not simply to their own families or to other people who believe the same way they do. Positive faith communities strive to be more than Christian ghettos that provide alternative subcultures to those who find the "world" distasteful.

Unfortunately I run into a lot of Christians who want their church to be just that, particularly when it comes to their children and teenagers. They want the church to provide fall festivals for their children so they don't have to participate in Halloween. They want their church to provide a school for their children so they don't have to be in public school with the godless teachers. They want their church to provide Christian concerts for their teens so they won't want to go see those rock groups with interesting lifestyles and provocative lyrics. What they don't seem to understand is that being the salt and light Jesus talked about means being out and about in the world and understanding culture, not hiding from it.

Communities that value being salt and light and the good in the world God gave us to enjoy are the ones most conducive to soul care of children. Communities that see their primary purpose as shunning the rest of the world or protecting their members from the world only serve to create an "us versus them" mentality and do little to bring about the kingdom of God in our world. Instead they create a lot of people who think they are better than others because they follow Jesus. That's not citizenship. That kind of thinking does not love the world in the way God does or in the way Jesus commanded us to. And it's not conducive to creating positive faith development in our children.

In graduate school I read an interesting study about the moral development of adolescents. The researchers were intrigued that the number of teens who shoplifted from a Woolworth's in Greenwich, Connecticut, was so much higher than the number from a comparable Woolworth's store in the Boston area. They studied groups of teens in both towns to see if they could come up with anything that could account for the difference in their attitudes toward shoplifting. The only difference between the groups was that the teens they surveyed in Boston attended a private school in the city. To get to school they had to ride public transportation. These daily trips on the buses and subways put them in contact with different kinds of people and neighborhoods. The students living in Greenwich, on the other hand, never had to leave Greenwich. Unless they were intentional about it, they never ran into people of a different color, race, or economic background. The researchers of this very small study concluded that there is something about being with people different from yourself that promotes positive moral development.

What this study says to churches is that if we truly want our children to be people of faith who follow the ways of Jesus, we need to work hard at helping children be part of the world. We need to be intentional about helping them respect people who are different from them and helping them understand that part of being a faithful person is being concerned about the larger, extended community and the world. If we think that cloistering our children in a Christian ghetto will make them into God's people, we are sorely mistaken. But by being a community that models concern and care for the rest of the world, by involving our children in that care and concern, we can help our children become people of faith.

I said in an earlier chapter that for much of my career in children's ministry, I have worked with children I would characterize as children of privilege. They don't know they are children of privilege because everyone they go to school with and everyone in their neighborhoods have the same possessions they have or more. So they assume this is what normal life is all about. These children have a hard time understanding that they live better and more affluently than most of the people in the world. And I think this makes it harder for these children to follow Jesus. After all, why does a person need Jesus when he has more toys at home than he could possibly ever play with and he's never gone without a meal or an after-school snack?

These children need a community that, while thankful for its affluence, is a responsible steward of it. These children need a community where following Jesus is not just about what Jesus does for me or what God provides for me, but where the community understands that following Jesus has more to do with what I can do for others and the rest of the world. These children need a community that offers them (and their parents) opportunities to meet people from different cultural and economic circumstances. These children need a community that offers them opportunities to act as citizens of the kingdom of God in the whole world God made.

Our church has participated in World Vision's 30 Hour Famine as a way of sensitizing our children, teens, and adults to the issue of world hunger. During that weekend I suspend our usual children's educational programming in order to provide experiences that teach our children about world hunger and the need for generosity. Last year during Lent our church used the worship services to talk about the AIDS epidemic in Africa, health and hunger issues in rural Peru, and the needs of the poor in Minneapolis, offering members of our community opportunities to be involved in service in each of those areas.

Four times a year our church hosts homeless families. We create cozy "bedrooms" in our elementary classrooms where the families can stay for a week while they are trying to find work and homes. Several of our community's families come over to the church in the evenings so their children can play with the children in these homeless families. This not only meets the social needs of the homeless family but also gives the children in our church the opportunity to know children different from themselves. This activity provides church parents with a living object lesson to teach their children about homelessness and how Christians should respond to this issue and other social issues.

One family in my church community finds ways to involve their children in working with inner-city community agencies and churches. They are also intentional about taking their children to ethnic restaurants in not-so-safe parts of the city so their children can experience different cultures and people of different economic means. Faith communities that promote this type of citizenship are faith communities conducive to the spiritual growth of their members.

Story

Steve Sandage found that the last way in which communities provide positive faith experiences is through story. Spiritual formation happens when communities of faith communicate both their shared story and God's story through symbols, art, music, ritual, or written and verbal narratives. These communities have the ability to center their emotional connection to memories of a common history and the ways in which this history interacts and intersects with God's story. They are churches that understand that part of their purpose is to tell and retell God's larger, transcending story. They understand the importance of weaving all of our personal stories and histories into the fabric of God's story.

God chose to communicate with us through story. The Bible is a book full of stories that point to the character of God and God's plans for creation. We meet and understand each other and God through our own stories. Each community creates its own story of faith as it lives out God's story within its own culture and collection of community members. We come to know God through the stories God gave us, through the stories of people who have followed God through the centuries, and through the stories of those around us.

I was once part of a graduate level class in Spiritual Direction. During the first weeks of the class we were asked to create something that reflected our personal stories and their intersections with our spiritual lives. I found it fascinating and spiritually uplifting to hear the stories of these women and to hear and see the ways God was woven into the tapestries of their lives. Each story was different and powerful, and each story was a moving spiritual experience for me. God comes to us in the power of The Story as we share our own personal stories with others.

Children are not born knowing any of these stories or knowing they have a story to create. Stories are communicated to them by the older generations of the community, and the stories must be communicated to children in meaningful ways. Children must be taught to understand and verbalize their own stories as means of positive spiritual growth. Reflecting on one's own story of life with God helps one to see the work of God in one's life.

Last year I experimented with the power of story with a group of fourth and fifth graders. I wanted them to understand the importance of their own stories and the stories of others in their understanding of God and of living in the way of Jesus. We started out by sitting on the floor. I told the group my story of faith, and they seemed interested. Then I offered them the opportunity to tell their stories of life with God. I had several different types of creative media spread around the room that they could use to express whatever part of their story they wanted to tell. The children were invited to write their story using one of several laptop computers in the room, or they could make a collage from magazine pictures, or they could paint a picture of their story.

To get them started I offered a list of questions about their life with God. They were allowed to use these questions to help them tell part of their story. I gave them about 20 minutes to work on these projects, which most of them entered into with enthusiasm. At the conclusion of the work time the children were asked to sit down on the floor with their finished products. Each was invited to tell her story using the product she had written or made. They were not coerced to talk but allowed to pass if they weren't ready to share their story with the group. Most elected to share their stories, and it was fascinating to hear the realization of God's work in their young lives. During the last few minutes of our time together I read them the story of the life of St. Patrick. They were riveted.

The next week we tackled part of God's story in the Bible. When the kids arrived, I invited them to draw a picture representing their favorite Bible story on a long piece of butcher paper taped to the wall. Much to my surprise they entered into this task with much the same enthusiasm they'd shown the previous week. After they were finished with their drawings, I asked each one to describe in turn which Bible story he had picked, why he'd chosen it, and why he thought God wanted this story included in the Bible. Again I was surprised by the way these children articulated why a certain Bible story had power for them in their lives and by the thoughtful responses about God's purposes in how the story was given. I finished the evening with a modern parable of the Atonement, which again captured their imaginations and helped them think of Jesus' sacrifice in a new and different way.

This year I included a segment named "Our Story" as one of the activity centers in our Sunday morning program for first through third graders. This activity center was programmed with three segments reflecting the story of our church and the story of the universal church. For the inaugural segment I invited a woman who is a longtime church member and former staffer to tell the children the story of our church—how it started, why it started, and how we got to where we are today. For other segments I invited adult members of the community who don't usually spend time with these children to share their personal stories of faith.

We also did activities that helped us understand the stories of people who've been part of the church through the centuries. For example, during the Christmas season we explored the stories surrounding the historical Saint Nicholas.

Story is the way God chose to reveal spiritual mysteries to us. Story is the way we learn about each other and our own spiritual journeys. And it is through story that faith communities explain themselves to others. Caring for the souls of our children means sharing God's story with them in creative and appropriate ways. It means sharing our own stories of faith with them in age-appropriate ways. It means helping them understand their own stories. And caring for the souls of our children means incorporating them into the story, the shared experiences and memories, of the faith community.

Bring in the Children

A vibrant faith community that values integrity, acceptance, citizenship, and story—and accepts children as valid and important members of their fellowship—is an essential part of the children's spiritual development. But faith communities need to be intentional about including children in their activities and in their stories. Individual members of faith communities need to be intentional about developing relationships with children and about finding ways to work with children rather than always thinking they need to do things for children.

My church stands in a tradition that baptizes infants. Baptism is understood to be a rite that welcomes the child into the community. It is meant to involve the entire covenant community and not just the child's parents, extended family, and close friends. Baptisms are held during corporate worship services. The symbolism is that the entire faith community is coming around this family and this child as support, as people who have a responsibility to help this child grow in the Spirit and be faithful to God. In our service of baptism, the community vows end with the phrase "for they belong to us as well."

The gathered faith community takes a vow before God to share responsibility with the parents for the spiritual nurture of that child, and I believe those vows spoken before God need to be taken as seriously as marriage vows. Unfortunately, this is not usually the case. Those gathered in the worship service mouth the words of the vows, giving little thought to what they mean and what they are actually vowing to do. So I have undertaken a deliberate campaign to continually remind members of our community that if they say those words during baptisms, they have a duty to live up to them. Even dedication ceremonies include a vow from the congregation to support the spiritual development of that child. Communities need to be continually reminded of this responsibility.

If you are in children's ministry, you know it can be incredibly difficult to find willing, committed volunteers to work with the children. What a shame that the adults in our churches can't see the importance of connecting with the children in the community! The friendships children form with those who lead them in religious education are among the most influential relationships they will have in the community.

When I arrived at my current church, I knew that one way we could provide a total community experience for our children was to have a staff of volunteers that "looked like Colonial Church." This meant that we needed to recruit people into our children's ministries from all the generations in our community, not just those who are parents of young and school-age children. Each recruiting season we've been intentional about inviting people of all ages to be involved in teaching our children. And each year we've gotten closer to our goal of having a group of volunteers that spans the generations.

We use a small group format for most of our educational programs. The adults and teens who're our small group leaders have no other jobs except to build relationships with the children in their small groups. I give them tools to help them talk with the children, and we program small group time into our Sunday morning educational activities as a way to allow interaction to happen. These small groups also help the children build peer relationships within the church. A group setting of seven to eight children (fewer for preschoolers) is ideal for helping children know each other and discover each other's stories. Small groups are also ideal for helping children find their way and feel like they belong in the larger faith community.

While church growth and megachurch are still the buzzwords of modern evangelicalism, smaller really is better when it comes to children. In *Will Our Children Have Faith?* John Westerhoff writes that faith communities most conducive to the positive soul care of their children are those with no more than 300 members. While statistics show that most American churches are smaller than that, the bulk of the children who attend church are involved in communities with at least 300 members. If you are a full-time minister or director of children's ministries, you probably wouldn't have your job if your church was smaller than 300 members. But I think Westerhoff does have a point about larger numbers dissipating the spiritual effectiveness of community.

Most large churches understand that it's impossible to know and care for a large group of people, so they work hard at promoting small groups as a means of finding biblical community in the midst of a large and perhaps overwhelming group of people. This concern for the smaller group and the importance of the relational aspect of the smaller group does not always trickle down to the way we handle our children's ministries. Finding children's ministry volunteers is difficult, and large churches are loath to cancel children's ministry programs for lack of volunteers. So many of these programs stumble along with lots of children and few volunteers, putting a strain on the volunteers' patience and classroom management skills. The chaos and lack of personal attention that ensues can create an untrustworthy environment for children, causing them to have less-than-stellar opinions of church. Worse yet, it can steal from them the opportunity to participate in the life of the faith community and build relationships with adults and with each other.

Some churches combat this problem by simply entertaining large groups of children on Sunday mornings or Saturday nights. They put lots of time and money into creating Disney- or Nickelodeon-worthy entertainment. The children are entertained for an hour and hear a moral lesson, and there is little need for volunteers other than those who put on the entertainment each week. (This, of course, is tons more fun for the volunteer than wiping runny noses and dealing with discipline problems.) While these kinds of big-production ministries certainly attract children, the children are never offered the opportunity for any kind of interaction with other generations or intentional, guided interaction with each other. This is not good for kids emotionally or spiritually.

In fact, a recent report from the Commission on Children at Risk argues that the loss of connectedness is devastating America's youth in a host of ways.

The commissioners, many of them physicians and mental health professionals, say they believe that human beings have an inborn need for connections, first with their parents and families, then with larger communities. It is, they say, the weakening of the connections between children and their extended families and communities that is producing a virtual epidemic of emotional and behavioral problems.[2]

The report goes on to discuss the need for authoritative communities, places that are warm and loving but also exhibit reasonable expectations and limits. These communities work best when a number of generations are involved in providing support and nurture as well as moral and spiritual meaning. And they work best when they are small.

The relationships children have with others in the community seem to facilitate behavioral changes in the children. As the report makes clear, "Good behavior is at least as much the result of relationships as of rules. The relationships are the source of the thing we call conscience, without which rules are only as strong as the ability of the rule makers to enforce them. Relationships are key."[3]

If what this report says is true, then churches are in a wonderful position to be these authoritative communities. As communities of faith we already believe in the importance of relationships and belonging. We have the chance to connect our children with others and across the generations in meaningful ways. In doing so we affect not just psychological health but spiritual health as well. The relationships children find in a community of faith are crucial to their spiritual development. These relationships are integral to their ability to find spiritual meaning in a life with God.

Notes

1. The author is indebted to Steven Sandage's (along with Carol Aubrey's and Tammy Ohland's) thoughts on community both from personal conversation and the article "Weaving The Fabric of Faith," *Marriage and Family: A Christian Journal,* Volume 2, Issue 4, 381 –398.

2. From WashingtonPost.com article by William Raspberry, "Environmentally Challenged," September 22, 2003.

3. Ibid.

six

The Family Factor

Family is everything to a child. Family is the first place a child forms and experiences relationships. It is a child's first experience of community. Family is where a child learns language and motor skills and where she develops her first view and understanding of the world. Family is the first place a child experiences love, intimacy, forgiveness, and physical care. Conversely, family can also be the place where a child experiences her first emotional violence, neglect, indifference, and physical hurt.

We can never get away from our families. We may leave them physically. We may move miles and miles away from them and never have any contact with them again, but we can never really leave them. Our families leave a permanent image on our lives that affects everything we do. Whether it be a physical resemblance to a parent, an attitude about politics, or a way of roasting a turkey, our experiences with our families mold us for life and turn us into the people we become.

With that in mind I don't think it's an exaggeration to say that family is the most important arena for a child's spiritual development and soul care. Even families who never attend church nor consider issues of spirituality and ethics in their decision-making are spiritually forming their children. They are teaching their children that these things don't matter in the same way that families who do seek out lives of faith teach their children that these things do matter.

The developmental stages and crises purported by Erikson happen primarily in the context of the family. As we know, it is in the family that a child learns the trust of others that is so important in learning to trust God. The family is where the child learns to see himself as lovable and competent and develops the positive self-image he needs to understand God's love for him. The family models for the child what it means to follow Jesus and love God and what it means to work through spiritual struggles and failings.

With that in mind it seems obvious that anyone who wades into the waters of child rearing should take the responsibility very seriously. But that seems not to be the case, particularly for those who populate the church world. One would think with all the talk about family values the church has spewed out over the last two decades that most, if not all, churches would take seriously the importance of family in the spiritual nurture of their own children. One would think that churches would work hard at empowering parents to model faith at home and to use teachable moments and intentional practices to positively nurture their children in spirituality. One would think that would be the basis of children's ministry. But that's not the case at all.

The Broken Family

Most children's ministries, particularly in large churches, hardly take the child's family into account. Most children's ministries segregate the children in age-level groups, providing teaching and activities for them while the adults go off to do "adult" things.

During my first months as the children's pastor at a megachurch, the senior pastor asked me to evaluate how I thought the church as a whole viewed the role of children's ministry in the overall mission of the church. I told him that the impression I had was that the adults, particularly the influential leaders of the church, thought they had a good children's ministry when the children were being told Bible stories quietly in the basement of the church building while the adults were doing the important work of God upstairs. This pastor told me that my evaluation was accurate, and I'd say that's still the prevailing attitude about children's ministry at that church.

The bias at most churches seems to be that real church is for adults only. The norm is to segregate families by age so that parents and children are never together once they walk in the front door. So it should come as no surprise that parents leave the church building each week with few tools to help them care for the souls of their children.

The modern church also tends to see children's ministry programming as support for adult ministry programming, not as something important, nurturing, and helpful to families in and of itself. The following scenario is common in many church staff meetings. Those responsible for adult programming want to offer a special program or class. The question that always arises is, "But what will people do with their children?" So everyone turns and looks at the children's pastor and says, "You can provide childcare or a class for these children, can't you?"

It doesn't matter if the time frame is good for children. It doesn't matter that this is one more time the church is separating families. It doesn't even matter that it could be difficult to recruit enough adult volunteers to give these children a safe and trustworthy environment. What matters is that we've given the adults someplace to put the kids so they can satisfy their own personal spiritual cravings and interests. Then, often, the fact that this children's program exists is used as a marketing tool to attract adults to the program or to the church. Many large churches talk about having good age-related, segregated children's programs because this attracts adults to their ministries. The large attendance numbers these churches crave are built on programs that have little to do with the soul care of the children, little to do with supporting families, and everything to do with giving the consumer what he wants.

This proliferation of age-segregated programming and the understanding that children's ministry programming often exists to promote adult programming have led the church to propagate two fallacies to parents. First, churches tell families that it's okay to expect the church to take care of their children every time the doors are open. By doing this we turn our children's ministry staffs into highly educated baby-sitters. We also create a sense of entitlement within our community that says the church exists to serve its members and not the other way around. I do believe that parents need a break from their children, particularly those parents who have multiple preschoolers. However, I don't believe it is the responsibility of the children's ministry to provide more and more children's religious education programming to meet that need. I don't believe it is the primary job of the children's minister to give people a place to leave their children so they can talk with other adults.

At the same time I do believe it is a community responsibility to offer respite for those parents who are weary of parenting and who feel they will go insane if they don't have a conversation with someone other than a two-year-old soon. This is one way members of the faith community can care for each other. One emerging church I am familiar with does not offer traditional nursery care during its worship gatherings, believing that even the cries of infants are pleasing to God. But this church also realizes that some parents are uncomfortable if their baby starts to make noise (purely a Western cultural taboo, I believe) or really can't concentrate on what's happening with a squirming baby in their arms. So they have created a community volunteer position called "Baby Holders."

Prior to the beginning of the worship service these volunteers watch for people who come in with babies and offer to hold the babies at any time during the service. These people are always in the same room as the parents, in clear view, so there is no concern about something untoward happening to the children. There is also a room located off the worship area, in full view of the worship area, where a parent can take a child who is on a crying jag and still feel a part of the worship experience. Emerging communities will wrap themselves around families and offer them help with their children. They will not depend on more and more children's programming to make it happen.

The second fallacy promoted by churches heavy on segregated children's programming is that the church can do the spiritual nurture and soul care of children better than families can. This is simply not true. The average child is involved in church programming for, at the very most, 150 hours out of the year (and that's for families who are at church every time the doors are open). When you contrast that with the countless number of hours a child spends within his family each year, it almost seems incredulous that anyone could believe the church can do a better job of spiritual nurture than families can.

But that is exactly what churches are telling families with their major emphasis on children's educational programming and little to no emphasis on helping parents train their children in the faith and nurture their burgeoning spirituality. By doing this, the church is shortchanging families and children. Churches who tell families that the church can do spiritual formation better are usurping what I believe to be a parent's God-given responsibility and gift: to care for the souls of their own children. They are taking on a responsibility no program can ever fulfill.

The Family Tradition

When you look at the entire scope of the Bible, it really doesn't have much to say about families, parents, or even children. The Bible was never meant to be a handbook on Christian child rearing. One thing we need to remember when looking to the Bible for advice about the nurture of children in families is that the family culture of Old Testament times was very different from the family culture of 21st-century North America. The family culture of New Testament times was very different from both that of the Old Testament—mostly Middle and Near Eastern cultures—and the family culture of 21st-century North America.

Families in Old Testament times were not the separate, independent, nuclear families of our day. They were part of a larger, extended tribal structure where men and women had clearly defined roles for family life. There was always an older sister or extended family member to take care of the children when the mother was incapacitated or busy with other things. Because this was not necessarily a highly literate culture, the primary modes of communicating were the spoken word and songs used in the retelling of the history of the people. Celebrations and feasts were designed to be visually symbolic of the event celebrated so that even the children, who were included in all of the community's events, could understand the story just by participating in the festival.

The most oft-quoted piece of child-rearing advice found in the Old Testament is in Deuteronomy 6: the parents are instructed to tell God's story to the children when they are walking and lying down, instructed to take every opportunity daily life offers to tell and retell the story of God's goodness to the people and the covenant promise he made with them. I still find this ancient passage to be helpful to parents today for two reasons. First, in giving this command to the Israelites, God was reinforcing the idea that parents are in the best position of anyone to communicate the things of faith to their children. Second, it shows us that God understands the old adage that faith is more caught than taught. The best faith education is informal. The best faith education comes from asking God to be present in all the everyday, mundane acts of life as well as the monumental and life-changing ones.

The New Testament, like the Old Testament, offers little enlightenment on child rearing and the soul care of children. New Testament families, while more urban and cosmopolitan than the tribal and agrarian families of at least the pre-exilic Old Testament, were still very much based on the extended-family concept. Many members of the family might live in one household in both the Greek and Roman cultures of early Christianity. Gender-specific roles in the family were still fairly well defined, but women were merchants and lawyers and did participate more and more in the civic life of the community. No biblical accounts of early church life mention children or the segregation of them into their own churches, leading me to believe that they were probably included in the worship, meals, and other activities of the fledgling church.

New Testament writers were gravely concerned with the faith communities developing around new believers in the work of Jesus. They wanted to help new believers understand what it meant to live together as followers of Jesus. They used the metaphor of the family to help the community live and operate like a functional family. So if spiritual growth is a communal, relational activity (and I believe the launchers of the early church thought this) and the community of faith is to model itself on the family, then it would seem that there is some biblical backing for the idea that the family is the first and foremost seat of spiritual formation for the child.

And so it is unbiblical for the institutional church to hijack this responsibility from families. Instead of building children's ministries on more and more programming, the church needs to see families as the axis of their children's ministries. The first priority of children's ministry ought to be supporting parents in their role as the primary spiritual nurturers of their children. The goal of children's ministry needs to be finding ways to help parents talk about spiritual things with their children and helping families prioritize and center their lives on God's presence. Tomorrow's churches need to capture the vision of the family as a sacred community.

The Family Church

We've already talked about the sheer amount of time children spend in families and how children experience every facet of life within their families, but there are other factors inherent in family life that allow families to be the center of soul formation for children. Roman Catholic educators call the family the "domestic church." It is the safe home where spirituality is formed, practiced, explored, and questioned in perhaps a more intimate way than can ever happen in even the best of faith communities. The home is a place where community spiritual practices can be honed and reflected in the nurturing environment of the family. It is a place where faith can become our own in the whirl and storm of everyday life, a small, important microcosm of the larger community of faith.

The Refuge

In *Family: The Forming Center*, Marjorie Thompson describes several models of the family that speak to its ability to spiritually nurture its children.[1] One such model is the family as sacred shelter. Thompson uses Dolores Leckey's description of the family when she describes it as, "a place of acceptance, nurture, and growth that empowers family members to participate...in God's ongoing acts of compassion and salvation."[2] For the child the family should be the safest place on earth. It is the only place where he can be absolutely who he is and still know he will be accepted and forgiven. In the family the child can express all that he is feeling and desires to do and be without fear of being cast out. While the family may not deem all of these actions and desires appropriate, the family will still show the child unconditional love and acceptance, allowing the child to grow emotionally strong and confident in his own abilities. This acceptance of the child's identity, feelings, and actions by the family will mirror to the child the love and acceptance God feels for him, helping that child to fully experience God's love.

The family provides a child with affirmation of her gifts, abilities, and personality that, in turn, helps her see herself as lovable and competent. Hanging finger paintings on refrigerator doors, praising those first tentative steps, providing age-appropriate and respectful behavioral expectations administered with unconditional love, being an encouraging presence at soccer games, and naming a child's delightful and endearing qualities are just some of the ways parents help their children develop healthy self-esteem and personal confidence. The family's affirmation of the child's personhood and abilities will speak to God's affirming presence in her life and help her understand that she is loved by God as a part of God's glorious creation.

Families provide accountability for children in a non-threatening atmosphere. Families can model for the child what right and just relationships look like. As children learn to live with siblings and watch their parents relate to each other, they learn how to live in intimate relationships with other people. Parents help children sort through the storms of living with a difficult brother or sister. Parents can hold a child responsible for right or wrong actions taken in a familial relationship. This teaching helps the child learn how to live in relationships outside the family, which prepares the child for right living within the community of faith and in the world at large.

Part of learning how to live in relationship with others is learning how to forgive. Jesus and the writers of the Epistles talk a lot about forgiveness. Just as God has forgiven us, we are to forgive others—both inside and outside the family. Thompson defines forgiveness as "making a conscious choice to release the person who has wounded us from the sentence of our judgment, however just or fair the judgment."[3] Learning about and practicing forgiveness, a huge part of spiritual maturity, simply cannot be taught in a classroom.

True forgiveness costs us something. If a relationship means very little to a child, then the act of giving or receiving forgiveness in that relationship will also mean very little. But when children see their parents forgive each other, when they are given the gift of forgiveness from a parent or sibling, or when they have the opportunity to forgive a parent or a sibling, they grow in understanding of the meaning and power of forgiveness. Everyday family life offers a myriad of opportunities, both major and minor, to practice forgiveness and discover God's great gift of grace.

While the church community can—and certainly should—be a safe haven for children, it simply cannot compare with the sheltering safety of the family. Families provide unique models of God's love, justice, and forgiveness. The safety of families allows children to experiment with feelings, questions, and ideas as they learn to follow in the way of Jesus.

The Storykeeper

Thompson also defines the family's role in spiritual formation as that of storyteller and guide. The model for this is found in the Old Testament book of Deuteronomy (the passage discussed earlier in this chapter). According to Thompson, the family has three stories to tell. First, the family has personal stories of faith and life to share with the child. All children love to hear the story of the day they were born. Parents can tell this story over and over, each time bringing God into the midst of that special day. Parents and grandparents can share the stories of how they came to love God and Jesus. They can tell stories about ways in which the larger community of faith has been important to them over the years.

Second, families share the stories of their past, giving children a sense of the history, continuity, traditions, and stability of their family. Children like to hear stories of when Grandma, Grandpa, Mom, and Dad were their age. They enjoy hearing what it was like to grow up in a different era and are often incredulous to learn that people actually lived without computers, Game Boys, and minivans. These stories not only entertain children, but also give them a sense of being part of something lasting, something strong and secure.

Finally, families tell the biblical stories that have been passed down through the generations of God's people. When Bible stories are told to children in a family setting, they are told as what they are—stories. Most parents don't close out a Bible story with a sermon. Instead children are allowed to hear the story, play with it in their minds, and draw their own conclusions from it. Family is perhaps the only place children hear God's story with little commentary or polemicizing. Children need to first hear God's story before they can live in God's story. Hearing the personal story of family and God's story within the family helps them do just that.

Here again the church certainly has an obligation to tell these stories and to create places where children can find their place in the broader story of the community. But it is in the family where the concept of story as a means of formation really gels. Families have the ability to tell God's story and their own story spontaneously. Families can tell stories that fit specific circumstances. They can tailor the story to meet the needs of the child or the situation. Families can tell the stories over and over again, and generally speaking, no one (except perhaps a preteen) complains about having heard this story too many times. Many stories become the fabric of a family's life together. And while members of a faith community do create stories together, families have much more opportunity to create their own stories around and about their faith and faith experiences.

The Servant

As I mentioned earlier, there is a communal nature to citizenship, a responsibility to care for the people and things God created. If this understanding is instilled in the child through family life, it will be a natural transition for the child to carry this kind of citizenship into the community of faith.

Service is an essential element of healthy family life. In order to maintain a home, each person in the family must share in the various tasks necessary to keep life running smoothly. That might mean one child has to clean up the toys left out by the other children. It might mean one child has to clear the dishes of everyone else in the family. Family life means serving one another by taking out the garbage and loading the dishwasher. It means sacrificing what I want because someone in the family wants something else. These daily efforts at serving and sacrificing lay the groundwork for the life of service to which our faith communities call us.

Families are well suited to teach children about stewardship, not just the giving of monetary resources, but as an understanding of how God wants us to treat all the resources of our world. But our attitude toward money is a big deal. The way we understand and use money typically comes from early attitudes built in our childhoods. Christian parents interested in the soul care of their children have a marvelous and awesome responsibility to model and teach their children about generosity toward others and about how our generosity helps to create God's kingdom on earth. This requires that parents look hard at their own attitudes toward money and generosity. If money is a god to them, then money will be a god to their children, no matter how many Sunday school lessons the child sits through.

The family also has a powerful ability to foster acceptance and love of others in their children. If a parent shows disdain for the poor, then it is extremely likely the children of that family will hold the same opinion. If the family only spends time with people like themselves because they are scared of people who are different, then it is likely the children will develop an attitude of superiority to those who do not hold the same moral or religious views the family does. I've heard many stories about children and teens who attend Christian schools and look down on neighbors and other friends who aren't part of the crowd that knows the truth. To be spiritually mature means to love the world as Jesus does; it is to love outside of the boundaries of race, economics, or privilege. The family is crucial in developing the child's ability to do this.

Actively reaching outside the home to help those in need teaches children what it means to live life in service to others. This might mean involving the family in works of mercy and caring or in works of justice. Each year at Christmas time my church sponsors the Giving Tree project. At the beginning of Advent, the Christmas tree is full of gift tags suggesting gifts for people helped by a specific mission or social service agency in our area. One year we bought toys for the children at an inner-city church. Another year we put together gift boxes of toiletries and gloves for homeless men and women in our city. Families are asked to pluck a tag off the tree and together purchase the items suggested on the tags. Then they bring the gifts back to the church building and place them under the tree. Each year we have an overwhelming response.

I once asked our Children's Ministry committee if we should take a break from this project and think about doing something else. I was met with a resounding "no" from everyone present. While purchasing a gift for the Giving Tree is not a sacrifice for most families, in a small way it does get families thinking and talking about caring for and serving those who are less fortunate than they are. Hopefully it creates a hunger to help and paves the way for bigger and better opportunities for families to serve together.

If as churches we desire to see families take back their rightful place as the center of soul care and spiritual nurture for their children, we must give them tools to do this. If families are indeed sacred shelters, keepers of the sacred story, and servants in God's world, then the church needs to come alongside to help them be these things.

A Place for Parents

Our church has started offering parent-child learning events that give parents and children shared experiences around Bible stories and the life of the community. The liturgical church year offers lots of opportunities to do this. Every year on the first weekend of Advent, our church sponsors a Family Advent Fair. Sunday school classrooms are set up with a variety of activities designed to teach about the meaning of the Advent season and to help families celebrate Christmas together spiritually. Families make simple Advent wreaths or calendars. Or they make a Baby Jesus doll to remind them of what this season of waiting is about. It's great fun to see these families working and talking together about God's gift to us. And because many of the items they make can be used to mark the days of the

Advent season, they have been given a way to talk about these ideas at home.

We also sponsor an Advent class for parents and grade-school children and one for families with preschoolers. Here again we talk about the special meaning of this season, and we make or experience something together that can be used throughout the waiting of Advent. Each Advent season we offer families an activity booklet full of ideas for celebrating Advent and Christmas in the home and devotionals to use around the family's personal Advent wreath.

The season of Lent, while not as festive as Advent and Christmas, offers opportunities for families to practice service, prayer, and penitence together as they prepare themselves for the central spiritual feast of Easter. We offer "Understanding Lent" classes for parents and their school-age children. One year we made butterfly trees. Together the families made both caterpillars and butterflies. All during Lent the caterpillars hung on the trees, then on Easter morning the caterpillars were exchanged for butterflies, symbolizing the new, beautiful life given to us in the resurrection of Jesus. In this class we've also made Lenten prayer charts where the family prays specifically each day for a group of people in their home, faith community, or world. Where I live spring break often falls during the season of Lent. One mom told me that her boys were so into praying through the prayer chart each week that they made sure the chart went with them on their spring break.

In an earlier chapter I mentioned our Shrove Tuesday pancake supper. One of the things we ask families to do around their tables is to make a decorative rendering of the "alleluia." Because it is a tradition in liturgical circles not to utter an "alleluia" during the Lenten season, we instruct our families to take their "alleluia" home, hide it, and then bring it out on Easter morning when the waiting is over and we can finally, after the six weeks of Lent, shout "alleluia" about the resurrection of Jesus. One family took this activity very seriously, making sure their three-year-old waited until Easter to say his "alleluia." During our first Easter service of the morning, when the minister was reading a Psalm filled with alleluias, this little boy could contain himself no more. "Alleluia!" he shouted in the loudest voice he had. Let me tell you that childish yet profound outburst of joy made my Easter! To me it's proof that children latch onto things that are experienced and emphasized at home.

Churches can also give parents tools for caring for the souls of their children at home through various rites of passage. Each year our church gives Bibles to our second graders. If a child is to receive a Bible, we require that the child and at least one parent attend a class about understanding and using the Bible. We talk about how the Bible was written. We learn interesting facts about the Bible. And we play games to learn how to find books, chapters, and verses in the Bible. Parents always walk out the door after the class and tell me how much they learned. For one family the class and the gift of the Bible fostered a special bedtime ritual for a father and son. This second grader was so excited about using his new Bible that he and his dad now read a few chapters together each night before bed—at the behest of the son.

Some churches experiment with bringing parents and children together in a family Sunday school as a means of helping parents transfer the learning and experiences garnered at church programs into the home. So strong is this belief that the church needs to come alongside families in spiritual nurture and not compete with them, that one emerging church in California offers an intergenerational

Sunday school experience as their only weekly educational programming. Faith Inkubators, an educational organization based in Stillwater, Minnesota, offers training for churches on how to implement the Family Sunday School, providing intergenerational curriculum and resources. Another California emerging church experiments with creating small groups that include both children and adults as a means of helping parents care for the souls of their children.

Often churches equate equipping parents with simply offering parenting seminars or classes. I think these can be helpful in motivating and aiding parents to understand their responsibility as the primary spiritual nurturers of their children, but they should not be the only equipping tool offered. I've sponsored workshops on understanding how children develop spiritually. The parents who attended told me they found it helpful and that they were sorely lacking in this area of understanding their children.

Our church has an informal fathering group that meets two or three times a year to discuss a book on parenting. I don't find that men get really excited about attending parenting workshops, but because this is for fathers only and does not require a great deal of time on their part (fathers are encouraged to come even if they have not read the book), men have attended and found it helpful. This group has also spawned several informal, non-programmed-by-the-church-staff father/child events such as cookouts and trips to professional baseball games.

In truth most parenting seminars are poorly attended. A popular psychologist/speaker friend of mine who packs out his speaking engagements all over the country has recently written a book on parenting. He was asked if he would turn this book into a parenting seminar the same way he had with his books on relationships and other topics. He said he doubted that he would because, in his experience, no one comes to parenting seminars. The lesson is that the last thing parents want from their churches is a parenting seminar. What they want and desperately need are creative ways to care for the souls of their children.

The tools we give parents needn't be complicated or costly. Often parents simply need help seeing the everyday opportunities that can help them teach their children about faith. They need to know that a beautiful sunset over the Pacific Ocean is a great time to talk with children about the beauty and creativity of God; a scary thunderstorm is a wonderful time to talk with children about how we can tell Jesus when we're afraid. These daily opportunities to enhance the faith understanding of children pass by parents because they haven't been taught to look for them. Or they get busy and tired, and God seems far away. It's impossible for parents who feel detached from God to pass God on to their children. Perhaps the best tool we can give to parents is to relieve them of the belief that this is rocket science. While the soul of a child is a tender thing, it is also ready to be filled with the joys and wonders of life with God. Most of the time all parents really need to do is pay attention and be intentional about shaping the faith of their children.

These days our church is looking for ways to provide families with books and other tools designed to help them bring spirituality to the center of their family life. The Augsburg Youth and Family Institute in Minneapolis publishes lots of fun, helpful nonbook resources for families to use together. For example, families and churches may purchase packets of "table talk" cards containing questions and topics for the family to discuss at meals or other times when the whole family is together. My hope is that our church will create a place for our parents to find and check out these and other resources to use at home. I'd like to see us develop mentor families who can build relationships with families who are just starting out, offering them the wisdom of their own struggles in the soul care of their children and modeling for them aspects of family life that nurture a child's spirituality.

Even these ideas can only go so far. Perhaps the most important time to set these wheels in motion is before a couple becomes parents. At my church I conduct a segment of our premarriage workshop on family spirituality where I help couples understand that the families they create will be the center of spiritual nurture for their children. I ask them to start considering questions of family traditions and time spent on spiritual matters in the home. I've discovered that, unless children are being brought into the marriage, most engaged couples have given little thought to the spiritual life of the family they will probably have. But discussion and planning about how the children will be nurtured and cared for spiritually needs to happen before children arrive. Once children are born, there is little time for those kinds of discussions.

As I've been writing this chapter, I've heard a little voice in my mind saying, "But what about kids who come to our churches without their families or kids that come from such dysfunctional situations that positive spiritual nurture is just a pipe dream for these families? Where do these kids get their souls cared for?" The simple answer is that their soul care must then come from members of the faith community. A child loses a lot in the way of positive spiritual nurture when the family is broken, in crisis, or spiritually indifferent. The child loses the valuable experience of faith lived out in the crucible of the family when everyone in the family is too preoccupied with life's problems to make the connection between life experience and life with God.

The faith community needs to be attuned to these children, to their particular situations and families, and be ready to do what is necessary to help these children and families feel enfolded into the community. Perhaps families can "adopt" these children into their own families—taking them under their wings during worship or other community events. Or maybe empty nesters or young couples without children can watch over these children, giving them a small taste of what is missing in their own families. But the community cannot neglect these children or families. It is our serious responsibility to watch over them.

It's also worth noting that as I've experimented with the family ministry events and ideas talked about in this chapter, the families who have offered the most enthusiastic response are those who are most likely to be immersed in the postmodern worldview and who are the parents of up-and-coming millennial and adaptive children. These generations seem to be hungry for family-centered events and are eager to include their children in all aspects of life in the community of faith. Children's ministry in the emerging church must focus on families as the center of a child's spiritual nurture and formation. The church cannot do right by its children without including families, but families cannot go it alone. Faith communities must partner with families, helping them understand their role in the soul care of their children and supporting them in this task. Only then will we see lasting spiritual growth and understanding in our children.

Notes

1. These characteristics are found in Marjorie J. Thompson's book, *Family: The Forming Center,* Upper Room Books, 1997.

2. Edwards, Tilden M., *Living with Apocalypse,* ed. Dolores Leckey, Harper Collins, 1984, 172.

3. Thompson, 65.

seven

The Bible Is for Children, Too

Last Christmas I scoured both Christian and large chain bookstores to find the Christmas story from the Gospel of Luke disguised as a children's book with good artwork. I wanted to use this during the Family Christmas Eve service at my church. I thought this would be easy to find. But out of all the Christmas books in print, I found only two that came close to what I wanted. Oh, I found variations on the story of the incarnation of God, but they all embellished the story by adding talking lambs or small children who just happened to be in the stable that night to hang out with Mary and Joseph and witness the birth of Jesus. I never believed it would be so hard to find the Bible story. Apparently (to bookstores at least), children will not find God's story interesting enough the way God gave it to us, so we have to make it better. I think my rather fruitless hunt for this book symbolizes the difficulty the current, modern church has with teaching children the Bible.

The Bible holds the story of God within its pages. The Bible is where Christians go for guidance. And the Bible is the book most Christian churches use to introduce children to faith in God. But study of the Bible is not without its questions and controversies.

The stories of the Bible were written a long, long time ago over a period of thousands of years. The cultural milieus of the Bible are very different from the culture of 21st-century North America, which often causes great misunderstanding of the biblical text and difficulty in passing on its message. The stories of the Bible were written originally in ancient languages, and the translation process always has been fraught with exegetical landmines and personal and theological biases. The men and women who wrote the stories of the Bible had no idea that we would be reading their stories and trying to explicate them to find some hidden truth God desires us to know. And since we all bring our own stories and our community's story to any reading of the Bible, we all read the Bible subjectively. There is never an objective exegesis or analysis of the biblical text. We'll never know for sure what the original writers of the story were intending to say. And this has implications for the way we use the Bible with the children in our care.

As if that weren't enough, those with a postmodern ethos view the Bible differently than those who view the world from a modern perspective. Earlier in the 20th century, teachers of the Bible could assume that the general population had some rudimentary understanding or knowledge of the stories of the Bible. Bible stories were a part of our secular and literary culture, and it could be assumed that most people had at least a belief in the God of the Bible and in the validity of the stories of the Bible. They may not have been trying to follow Jesus explicitly, but at least they knew who Jesus was.

This is no longer the case. Even young adults who've grown up in the church have little knowledge of the facts and details of the Bible. They don't get the biblical allusions found in poetry, novels, movies, or even television programs. And we can no longer assume that people believe in anything they think the Bible might say. They might believe some of what the Bible says and reject other pieces. They might validate another person's belief in the truth of the biblical story but not see it as relevant for themselves. Or they may be open to more intuitive and experiential interpretations of this ancient story rather than empirical, hermeneutical interpretations. Teachers of the Bible can no longer point to proof texts and think that people will simply believe it as truth because the "Bible tells me so."

How *Not* to Read the Bible

Unfortunately the 20th-century modern church's method of biblical interpretation has caused its people to lose a sense of the awe, mystery, scope, and majesty of the ancient texts by turning the Bible into God's answer book. Are you having a problem in your marriage? Read these Bible verses. Do you think you need to be a better father? Well, go to your local Christian bookstore and buy The Better Father's Bible. We continue to use the Bible this way when we teach it to children, robbing them of the wonder and awe contained in God's story. The Bible was not created as the practical guide to the Christian life. It is not a self-help book. The Bible is a collection of ancient stories in which an ineffable, powerful, and enigmatic God is the main character. The Bible reveals a God who is just as relevant today as 8,000 years ago—and just as powerful and just as mysterious.

These stories were not passed along orally and eventually written down to teach us an objective view of God and God's created world, but instead to show us a particular viewpoint on how God desires to interact with creation and how God wants the world to be. The Bible was given to us to promote a particular way of life growing out of the character of God. The Bible is to be the lens through which we learn to view our world and our place in it as people of faith. It is not simply a fact-filled textbook to be studied and from which to glean bulleted tips for a better sex life or for dealing with difficult people or even for ways to live a moral, antiseptic life.

When we use the Bible with children simply to teach doctrinal tenets, moral absolutes, tips for better living, or stories of heroes to be emulated, we stunt the spiritual formation of our children and deprive them of the valuable, spiritual story of God. When we only distill the Bible into practical applications and little life lessons, we fail to teach children how to use the Bible as a means of understanding God's overarching purposes in the world. We fail to give them the ability to understand their own stories in light of God's story. When we tell them what the Bible says or what to believe about what a particular Bible passage says, we rob them of the ability to experience the text for themselves and pull out its meaning in their own context and the larger context of their world. These are far more valuable spiritual skills for the child than learning Bible facts or spiritual axioms.

When we teach children the Bible simply to push forward a certain moral or theological agenda, we are guilty of what I call the "Aesop's Fableization" of the Bible. Literary history gave us moral fables. We don't need the Bible to teach children moral lessons. We need the Bible to introduce children to God, God's story, and God's ways. But I believe that most published Sunday school curricula are more focused on teaching children to be kind, obey their parents, and tell the truth (not bad things at all, by the way) than on helping children know God better. We use Bible stories with children as if they are moral fables given to us to teach a moral lesson!

For example, the story of the boy with the loaves and fishes is often used to teach children about sharing what they have with others. Children learn that Jesus was happy when the little boy was willing to share his lunch with the other people on the hillside. The take-home lesson is that if we share what we have with others, Jesus will be happy with us. But is that really what this story is about? Is this really why God decided to put this story in the Bible?

If we are to help children grow their souls, we need to teach them something more from the Bible than "Jesus is happy when we share." As we prepare to teach children Bible stories, we need to ask ourselves why we think God included this story in the canon of Scripture. Jesus and other Bible characters did lots of things in their lifetimes that didn't get included in the Bible. So if we believe that God had something to do with what the writers of the Gospels and the other books included in their narratives, we need to spend some time thinking about why these particular stories were included.

That's also a great question to ask children as we explore the Bible with them. Going back to our original story of the feeding of the 5,000 on the hillside, depending on which gospel account we read, this story has more to do with Jesus teaching his disciples something about himself and his mission than about the actions of the little boy with the lunch. So wouldn't it be more consistent with the sacredness of the biblical text to explore the person and purpose of Jesus as seen through the lens of this story?

When we teach children the Bible, we cannot forget the real protagonist of the Bible. We cannot forget that the Bible is primarily about God and God incarnate, Jesus, and God's plan for the redemption of creation. When we do, children walk away from our church educational programs thinking the Bible is primarily about Moses, Joshua, David, and Daniel. We treat Bible characters like the great heroes of history whose lives we should emulate. Jesus gets treated, not as God Incarnate, but as the greatest superhero of them all. We love to teach children about David's bravery and trust of God in the slaying of Goliath, but we rarely teach them about David's human failings and what they show us of God's character in God's choosing of David and his response to all of David's life.

We hold up Daniel as a paragon of loyalty to God's ways and the recipient of God's protection, but we rarely help children to see how the story of Daniel fits into God's plan for the Jewish people during the period of the exile and how Daniel helped to further these plans because he obeyed God.

We allow children to see the resurrection of Jesus at Easter, the centerpiece of the Christian faith, as the greatest act of any superhero. But we tend to gloss over the mystery of Jesus' presence on earth and the way in which his arrival ushered in a whole new chapter in the story of God's people.

By pulling stories about Bible characters out of the biblical text—which gives them no historical, cultural, or theological context—and by dwelling only on the exploits of the characters, we fail to give children the big picture of God's story in the Bible. We fail to help them see that the pieces of the Bible fit together in a wonderful tapestry of God's love and care for humanity and the rest of creation.

We also fail to give children a true picture of God's story when we sentimentalize the Bible for them. Many churches paint whimsical depictions of the story of Noah and the ark on the walls of their nursery and preschool rooms. Depictions of those cute, cuddly animals getting on that big boat two by two can be very appealing to young children. But the last time I looked at this story in Genesis, it's not a very cute, cuddly story. It's a story of God's displeasure with creation and God's desire to save it. Those animals and people were getting on that boat to save their lives—not to go on a floating zoo cruise to the Caribbean. And yet we continue to dwell on the animals and the rainbows and leave out the reasons for the boat and the rain. Are we afraid that God will lose face in the eyes of children if we tell the whole story? Are we worried that children will become scared of God if we tell the whole story? Or are we uncomfortable with the story ourselves? Perhaps we don't know what to make of this story, and so we really don't know what to tell children. So we twist it around to make it more palatable.

God is a God of grace, love, and forgiveness. God's whole character is alive and well in this part of the Noah story. We cheat children out of their knowledge of God when we are willing to only show them part of God's character. We give children a false view of God when we sentimentalize the Bible's stories of God for them. We sell short a child's ability to love and understand all of God's character when we shield him from the parts of God that don't seem so loving and graceful.

How Not to Teach the Bible

Another perennial problem with traditional Sunday school teaching Bible and traditional Sunday-school lessons found in both published curricula and in those churches that choose to write their own curricula is that the lessons and the teaching are rarely executed well. While it's good that people in churches are willing to give their time to teach children, too many of our volunteers have little understanding of how children think and learn and few classroom management skills. These gaps mean they can do little more than parrot back to the children the information in the teacher's manual. This approach rarely gives children the chance to let their own imaginations run with the story and never offers the opportunity to play with the story.

Lack of training, no knowledge of how children reason and learn, and little class preparation are a recipe for really bad Bible teaching. This does little to help today's children see the Bible and God's stories as relevant to their lives, culture, and ultimately the world. It's no wonder that surveys and polls of college students raised in the church show these students having little or no knowledge of the stories of the Bible and no way of making the intellectual, affectual, and behavioral leaps to see what living as a person of faith in God looks like in the real world and in their real lives.

Some churches attempt to make the stories of God relevant to children by using the Bible as a means of entertainment and fun. All one needs to do is peruse the covers of many children's Bibles and children's videos to see the fun cartoons and caricatures of Bible characters and Bible stories. Now there is nothing wrong with making the materials we use in teaching children colorful and eye-catching, but we do need to be aware of the message underlying these representations. If we are not careful, this can teach children that the Bible is not any different from their other storybooks and videos. When we show children the Bible as simply a book given for their amusement and entertainment, we may end up with children who have a view of God as the merry master (with Jesus as the erstwhile sidekick) of the universe who simply wants us to be cheerful, kind, and nice to other people. The stories of God are much more than that.

Many church-based children's Bible teaching programs consist of entertaining interludes that pass for religious education. The passive children sit watching puppets, skits, videos, and sleight-of-hand illusions based on the Bible, Bible stories, or Bible characters. The children may interact from time to time with what's happening onstage, or children may be called up front to participate, or they may get to jump around while singing songs about "pumping it up for Jesus." (What does that mean to a child, anyway?) Naturally children enjoy this, but I don't believe their spiritual lives or their experience with God is enhanced through these kinds of programs. There is little interaction with adult members of the faith community or the other children. There is no opportunity to wonder about or play with the Bible story. While these programs can seem wonderfully creative and child friendly, they do little to help children meet the God of the Bible and understand how to live as God's people.

How then should we share God's stories in the Bible with children? First, we need to always make our Bible stories about God, not about a political, theological, or moral agenda. We need to explore Bible stories with children in the whole context of God's story, asking why it was so important to God that humans know this story. We need to let them explore the story itself, asking, "What does this story tell us about God and God's plans for creation?"

When we use Bible stories simply to teach a life lesson, we dilute the power of the Bible to pique a child's curiosity and sense of wonder and awe about the mysteries of God. Instead we turn it into a pedantic book given to us simply to teach us right from wrong. No child is going to fall in love with that kind of book. We need not be so concerned with figuring out personal applications of Bible stories for children. Instead we can concern ourselves with the all-encompassing story of God for the world.

The truth is that those holding a postmodern worldview are not all that interested in being told what the Bible means for them. They are not eager to hear the three-point application of a Bible passage, reread the notes when they get home, and then act on it. (How much do those notes ever really get acted on, anyway?) Postmoderns want to know what the Bible says and then decide for themselves what they want to do with it. They want an open system of Bible study, not a closed one.

Letting the Scriptures Speak

When we share the Bible with today's children, we need to simply let the story stand. We need to tell children Bible stories, allow them to experience the Bible stories, and help them to get inside the Bible stories. When we tell children the great stories of children's literature, we don't give them a life application. Instead we let their imaginations play with the story, and we allow the story to speak to them in their own particular context. So why do we treat Bible stories so differently? In *Offering the Gospel to Children*, Gretchen Pritchard Wolff writes—

> We can rob this story of its power by telling it badly, by sentimentalizing or sensationalizing or distorting it, or by analyzing or reducing it to a theological formula, or a lesson to be learned to please the teacher. We cannot rob it of its power merely by telling it too often. It deserves to be told--over and over again, directly as gospel and liturgy, and also as it is mirrored in fairy tale, myth, and other works of art. And our children deserve the opportunity to respond to this story,

with clay, paint, and crayons, with their bodies and their voices, with their imaginations and their hearts, in worship, in sacrament, in celebration, and in play.[1]

As people responsible for the soul care of our children, we need to give them the opportunity to play with the story as a way to experience its power. Let's tell children the stories of God in the Bible and then give them the opportunity to work out the meaning for themselves.

Imagine what could happen if we allowed children—through the media of art, music, games, history, other stories (both personal and fictional), discussion, writing, and worship—to understand what God is saying in these stories. Imagine what could happen if we let God speak to children through Bible stories in ways that were meaningful to them. Let's not have a preconceived notion of what children should learn and do because they've had a Sunday school or Vacation Bible School lesson about a particular Bible story. By always thinking we need to explain and codify Bible stories with children, we usurp the power of God to speak through this extraordinary, living book given to us in love.

Just recently I developed a learning experience designed to help older elementary school children walk into and through the exodus of the people of Israel from Egypt. We explored some aspects of Egyptian life by experimenting with writing hieroglyphics and making jewelry similar to what Egyptians might have worn. We talked together about what life might have been like for Egyptians and what it might have been like to grow up in the palace of the Pharaoh. And we recounted together their previous knowledge of the story of Moses.

Then we explored the life of a Hebrew slave. We read, together, the first 14 verses of Exodus that describe how

God's people fell into slavery, some of the life of the slaves, and the Pharaoh's consternation with the prolific child-bearing of the Israelites. Then they were asked to personally consider what it might have been like to live the life of a slave in ancient Egypt. The children became quite engaged in this discussion, coming up with some interesting insights about what a life of slavery might have been like. After that we watched a video adaptation of the first half of the life of Moses. Then I asked each of the children to be silent for a minute or so (yes, they can do this) to reflect on the story they'd just witnessed and then asked them to share with me something that hooked them in the story. At no time did I attempt to explain the story or give them what I thought the meaning should be other than to explain some of the cultural allusions in the story.

One of the boys was struck by the determination of Moses' family to protect him from the death ordered by Pharaoh. Another child was amazed that the baby survived the journey down the river in the basket, citing perhaps the miraculous intervention of God. Never were these children asked to apply this story to their own lives or to pull out a spiritual lesson from the story, yet through various parts of the discussion and activities, they all did just that.

During the next session we looked at the second half of Moses' life—the story of the burning bush, the plagues, and finally the exodus of the Israelites from slavery in Egypt. As we talked about the burning bush event and the subsequent imposition of the plagues on the recalcitrant Pharaoh, the children initiated a discussion about how God acts in our world today. "Would God send plagues like those today?" they asked. They wondered, "What are the ways God deals with people who don't listen today?" I refrained from offering direct answers and instead asked them to reflect on their own questions and tell me what they thought the answers were. Then we explored the meaning of the exodus for God's people through the symbols of a Seder. One child asked why God would want the Hebrews to remember something that was so difficult and sad for them. This led to a discussion of what exactly God was asking the Hebrews to remember each time they celebrated the Passover.

At the end of our time together I asked the class why they thought God included this story of Moses and the Israelites' exodus from Egypt in the Bible. They responded with answers about the ways this story shows us God's love and God's power. These two sessions became powerful lessons about the nature and character of God, both in the past and today, where the children set the learning agenda themselves. My lesson plan enabled them to experience the story, but they pulled the lessons about God's character out of the story themselves with no prompting from me and without a formal "life application" section to the lesson plan.

Another way to help children explore and experience the ancient texts and stories of the Bible is by helping them understand and play with ancient spiritual practices of the church. One such practice is Lectio Divina, which literally means "divine reading." Lectio Divina can be described as a spiritual reading of scriptural texts where one listens with one's heart to what God has to say through a particular story. It is reflecting on the text of the Bible to be in contact with God. Simply put (and there are no set rules for Lectio Divina), one reads the text slowly several times over, allowing the words and phrases to enter into one's mind. Sometimes a word or phrase jumps out of the story, or a thought comes through, and one must take the time to respond to those words, phrases, or thoughts. Finally, Lectio Divina is a resting in the Word of God as we listen to God speaking to us at the deepest level of our being.

My children's ministry assistant and I have used Lectio with elementary-age children. Now we have no way of knowing what is going on in their heads as they reflect on the Bible story being read to them, but in my experience they do become engaged in the process and respond to the text without silliness and sometimes with profundity. Children can do silence. Children do not always have to be involved in hyperactivity in order to be engaged in the subject matter. And as they practice Lectio, I believe God speaks to them through the text of Scripture in ways that are meaningful to them because that is what God desires to do.

Another ancient spiritual practice is the Examen. This is a practice best done at the end of the day when the participants talk together about those things that happened during the day that sapped their zeal and energy, also known as desolations. Then they talk about those things that happened during the day that encouraged them or gave them energy, also known as consolations. At the end of the time we talk to God about all these things, bringing God into the very center of the important events of our lives.

For more than two years at my church, we have been practicing the Examen with elementary-age children during our Wednesday-evening educational programs. At the end of our sessions we sit in a circle on the floor with a candle in the center of the circle. I have been amazed at the way the children respond to this practice. Most participate (each person is allowed to pass if she doesn't wish to speak), and do so enthusiastically, sharing sometimes quite remarkable things about the good and bad taking place in their lives. And each week we explain as we go to prayer how God is involved and central to both the good things and bad things that happen in our lives. While there is not necessarily a direct teaching of the Bible when using the Examen (although there could be), it is another opportunity for children to experience the God they've just learned about in the stories of the Bible. As they talk about their lives, they know that God is just as relevant to them today as he was to those ancient people found in the text of Scripture.

Jerome Berryman, the director of the Center for the Theology of Childhood in Houston, Texas, is the founder of Godly Play, an approach to the religious education of children based on the thought and theory of Maria Montessori. Godly Play is a way of introducing children to the Bible and Christian themes. It invites children into God's story by encouraging them to wonder about God, themselves, and their world. Children are encouraged to play with Bible stories using their imagination and creativity to meet God on their own in powerful ways. Berryman writes that Godly Play "is a discovery method which engages the whole child—hands, heart, mind, senses, intuition" and "teaches reliance upon a gracious God who is real and accessible in all the mystery of life, both sad and joyful."[2]

Children hear the Bible story, play with it, wonder about it, hear it again (maybe in a different form), and discover meaning from it themselves rather than being told what it means. (We always remember things we discover for ourselves better than things someone has told us to believe.) Godly Play theory and practice take many forms in many different kinds of churches. Emerging churches might adopt the principles of Godly Play, or they might work with the idea of story, experience, and discovery in teaching children the Bible and then discover for themselves methods and content that work better for them and their own particular ethos. There is no single, foolproof way of introducing the living words of the Bible to children, but the concepts we've discussed can be helpful in setting a foundation for each church's unique educational focus.

In *Will Our Children Have Faith?* John Westerhoff outlines his ideas of what the teaching of the Bible to children should look like if today's child is to have a relevant, vibrant, and kingdom-building faith. He writes:

> Further, to be faithful to our historical, social, and cultural context, catechesis will need 1: to reaffirm the intuitive way of thinking and knowing, that is, to reaffirm the foundational roles of nature, the arts, and ritual in the lives of people; 2: To understand all of life as spiritual with two dimensions: one material, one nonmaterial; 3: To affirm that being and doing are one, but that doing proceeds from being; 4: To perceive all of life as a subject that engages us rather than as an object for our manipulation; thus, we return to the praying of Scripture as a complement to the study of Scripture; 5: To acknowledge that nature, history, society, and our personal lives are unmanageable and that we are communal beings dependent upon a God who is present and active in human life and history, a God with whom we can cooperate; 6: To acknowledge further that life is best understood as mystery and ordered freedom in which we are bound by relationships that make influence possible but not determinative; and 7: To know that there is only one end of human life (all else being means)— to live a life in an ever-deepening and loving relationship with God, to live a life that manifests itself in an ever-deepening and loving relationship with one's true self (the self in the image of God), with all people, and with the natural world.[3]

Some will criticize this view of teaching the Bible to children as one that fosters a low view of Scripture. Some will say that by disavowing the Bible as a book of propositions and truths to be learned, we are turning the Bible into just another man-made book of ideas that we can use or toss away depending on how we decide to live our lives. I would counter that this actually promotes a much higher view of the apartness of the Bible from other books. By centering our teaching of the Bible on the powerful stories of God given to us for the transformation of life, we are moving our understanding of the Bible from a dry book full of unquestionable morals and absolutes to a living, breathing, exciting book from which there is always something more to experience, understand, learn, play with, and think about. We are introducing our children to a relevant God who is passionately in love with them. Our use of the Bible should reflect this God and reflect our own transforming relationships with this God.

Notes

1. Pritchard, Gretchen Wolff, *Offering the Gospel to Children*, Cowley Publications, 1992, 14.

2. Berryman, Jerome, *The Complete Guide to Teaching Godly Play, Vol. 1*, Living the Good News, 19.

3. Westerhoff, John M., *Will Our Children Have Faith?* Harper and Row, 1976, 135.

eight

Children in Worship

When we first started experimenting with transgenerational worship in our church, the minister made an
attempt to make his sermons a bit more child friendly by
emphasizing story over application and abstract proposi-
tion. He told the story of Jacob, emphasizing what a
scoundrel he was. In the middle of the sermon, a three-
year-old girl in the congregation leaned over to her mother
and said of Jacob and his exploits, "He's going to get into
trouble." Let us never underestimate the ability of children
to understand in meaningful ways what is happening in
our corporate worship!

Participation in the communal worship of God is a crucial piece of human spiritual formation. This spiritual event
is the one time each week when the whole faith community—or at least a large portion of it—gathers together. I
believe there is something about joining with others in the

act of worship that strengthens our souls in both cognitive and affective ways. Unfortunately most churches exclude children from this community event and, therefore, exclude them from this important place of spiritual formation and soul care. For a variety of reasons children are shunted off to events and programs deemed more fun and age-appropriate than the worship of God with other seekers. By excluding children from corporate worship, churches have shortchanged them, denying them a weekly opportunity to express their faith and care for their souls.

John Westerhoff writes that if our children are to have faith, they must have opportunities to worship with the adults of the church. Worship is not only the time when the content of the faith is delivered, but also the time when churches communicate the feelings, subtle nuances, and transcendent meanings of the faith.[1] Participating with adults in the worship of God also helps children develop a sense of belonging to the community. It is through participating in worship services that a child develops her identity with the people of God and as a person of God. When children are involved in meaningful corporate worship, they experience the positive potential they have as children of God.

The worship experience is not only important for what it gives to children. Children contribute to worship in ways that are helpful to the soul care of the adults and teens who are present in the worship service as well. They contribute by their presence just as the adults contribute by their presence. A child's spontaneity and lack of inhibitions coupled with his inherent spiritual inclinations can add a dimension to corporate worship that is not found when children are excluded.

Since being part of corporate worship is so important to the spiritual formation of children and youth, it puzzles me that so many churches balk at including them in the worship service. Since children can make a substantial contribution to corporate worship, I wonder why more churches aren't figuring out ways to allow them to enhance their weekly worship of God. The big-picture answer is that most churches don't believe what I've just said in these last few paragraphs. Many churches don't treat their worship services as crucial vehicles for anyone's spiritual formation, much less the children. Many churches don't think it's all that important for children to feel a part of the whole community of faith.

I believe many churches have lost a sense of what the corporate worship of God is all about. It is no longer the centerpiece of community life, and this is reflected in how a church views the necessity of a child's participation in it. For many churches weekly corporate worship has become a variety show to be produced and enjoyed. The worship service's primary value is to be a slick entertainment vehicle where people leave the show feeling good about being at church. Anything that might make that show uncomfortable for people needs to be banned from it. Therefore, only the best musicians are allowed to perform. Singers need to smile brightly and dress in calming pastels and business-causal clothes. And there is certainly no room for a crying baby, a recalcitrant toddler, or a child who moves around the worship space or stands on the chair looking for a better view of the proceedings.

Children do make noise. Children find it hard to sit still. Children make it known when they are bored. Children do not have the inner restraints in social settings that adults do. So the inclusion of children in corporate worship does challenge many of our modern preconceptions of what worship ought to be. Several years ago our church made a commitment to being intentional about including children in our worship services. To prepare the congregation for this continuing experiment of transgenerational and child-friendly worship, I preached a sermon about the necessity of having the whole community together worshiping God as an act of spiritual formation. I challenged the congregation's understandings of what a worship service should be. I asked them who decreed that those participating in worship always had to be quiet. "I don't think it was God," I told them. I asked who it was who said there could be no moving about or changing places in worship. "I don't think it was God," I told them. So if the one we're worshiping is not concerned about these things, why are we?

Interestingly, the negative responses I got (there were lots of positive responses, too) were all along the same lines: "Having children in the worship service disturbs my worship of God." I find the operative word in that sentence to be "my." Worshiping God is not about us. Worshiping God is not about what we get out of it. Worshiping God is not about our feeling good when it's over. Worshiping God is about God and what pleases God. It is when we have that mindset that we are spiritually formed by worship. I think it pleases God when children worship, and I think it pleases God when adults welcome children into the worshiping community even though they can be noisy, disruptive, and uninhibited. Remember—God made them that way.

The Case against Children's Church

Caroline Fairless, an Episcopal priest, is a leader in the movement to involve children in corporate worship. She frames the whole issue as one of justice. Most of our churches would never exclude the physically or mentally disabled from our worship because they might be noisy or distracting. We don't send them off to a special worship service they can understand or fit into. In fact, most churches work hard to welcome disabled people into their communities. Yet we exclude children for these very reasons. They are noisy, cause distractions, and might not be able to understand what is going on.

But Fairless also acknowledges the difficulty inherent in convincing adults of the importance of including children in weekly community worship. She writes, "Resistance to full incorporation of children into the worshiping community is understandable. Their presence inevitably confronts the presuppositions about worship which have dominated liturgical practice."[2] Incorporating children into our corporate worship services is counter-cultural and disquieting, but churches truly interested in the soul care of their children need to grapple seriously with this issue.

That will mean rethinking what churches do in our worship services. Fairless suggests several questions churches need to consider when facing the question of complete inclusion of all community members in community worship. First, she asks churches to consider what scares them about including children in their worship services.[3] Are they afraid worship services will become out of control and unpredictable? After all, children aren't always under control and predictable. By including children in worship, we can't always control what will happen. (But we can't control God, either, so perhaps a little unpredictability during our worship services might allow God's spirit to move!)

Are church leaders afraid adults will be uncomfortable in a worship service where children are included as equal participants? I'm not sure the worship of God ought to be comfortable. I mean, we're worshiping the Creator and God of the universe. In worship we are coming before an everlasting mystery that loves us more than we can ever understand. We are in the presence of an all-powerful entity. I'm not sure there should be anything comfortable about that—comforting at times, perhaps, but not comfortable.

Are we afraid adults will leave our church if we include children in our worship services? Well, so be it. Part of the process of exploring the inclusion of children in corporate worship is helping people to understand how important it is for a faith community to care for the souls of its children and that including children in corporate worship is part of that care. We need to help adults get over their initial reluctance to worshiping side by side with children.

Are the ministers (and others) concerned that the sermon will become a less important part of the worship service? This may indeed happen when the meaningful inclusion of children in corporate worship is discussed and implemented! And this may not necessarily be a bad thing. Part of our rethinking of how we worship God in the postmodern church may well include rethinking the value of the cognitive, word-laden, auditory, 25-to-45-minute sermons. There might be other ways to share the stories of God during worship that will communicate with all worshipers better than a man or woman standing up front and simply talking.

This point leads Fairless to another question the church will need to ask: What happens to our churches when we dare to assume that children have the same claim on worship space, ritual, style, and content of worship as the adults? Truthfully grappling with this question may mean we need to rethink the way our worship spaces are designed as we create spaces with children in mind. Some churches in the United Kingdom have begun thinking seriously about the inclusion of children in their worship services. To provide children with space, these churches have removed a section of the pews in their sanctuary and replaced them with child-sized tables and carpeted activity areas. In these churches children are free to move back and forth between their parents or other adults and the quiet activities in their own special section. Likewise, when Solomon's Porch, an emerging church in Minneapolis, first began public ministry, the founders made a commitment to including children in their worship gatherings. So in their first worship space and in subsequent ones, they have included areas to help children both be involved in the worship of God and find activities to keep them occupied when their attention wanes.

Including children in corporate community worship also means that the style and content of our worship services may need to change so that it is meaningful to all the generations present. This more than redesigning the space can be a contentious discussion for churches. People become wedded to certain ways of worshiping and certain kinds of ritual until these means of worship become as important or perhaps more important than the object of worship. Changing the liturgy or order of worship to accommodate the needs of younger worshipers becomes tantamount, in some minds, to changing the words of the Bible!

We are installing a new sound system in my church's worship space. With this new sound system comes a video capability that necessitates state-of-the-art plasma-screen televisions mounted at the front. Our worship space is quite traditional and spare, modeled on the colonial Meeting Houses of New England. These plasma screens will give us the ability to make our worship more meaningful to a younger, more visually inclined audience. But to some people in our congregation the idea of video screens is anathema. They have made up their minds that they cannot worship God in a space that includes pictures and words illuminated on a screen that mars the colonial style of the room. The accoutrements of the room and the style of worship have become more important to these people than the worship needs of the whole community and, ultimately, the object of our worship—God—and what pleases God. Changing the ways we choose to worship God can be fraught with anxiety, anger, and dissonance; but if a church truly cares about its community and the soul care of children, it must not be afraid to address these issues.

The third set of questions proposed by Fairless regarding the inclusion of children in a church's weekly worship deal with the church's true view of its community. Churches need to consider what community truly means to them. What do we communicate about our sense of community when children and teens are not included in corporate worship services? A church that's working toward the meaningful inclusion of its youth in corporate worship is one that believes all ages are a part of the faith community.

Fairless then moves us to consider what the exclusion of children from worship says about our church's commitment to follow through on the vows made during infant dedication and baptism. I mentioned in an earlier chapter that during our infant baptism rite the community promises to teach the baptized children the stories of the Bible and help them to love Jesus because "they belong to us as well." Most churches have similar community vows included in either their baptism or dedication rituals. So if the community takes a vow to corporately care for the souls of its children and then excludes them from a meaningful, weekly experience of worship and spiritual formation, there is disconnect between what the community said it would do and what it is actually willing to do. How we act individually and corporately is a far better barometer of what we believe than what we say.

Fairless's final question for churches is a practical one: If children are never included in our community worship rituals and practices, how will they ever learn to value them? Over the years I have had many, many children tell me they don't want to go to "boring" church. Frankly, if I were a child who was asked to move from a setting that includes brightly colored sets, puppets, skits, high-energy songs, and perhaps even food fights to a staid worship service populated mostly by people who are not at all like me, I'd call it boring church, too. This attitude about corporate worship doesn't magically disappear at age 18. In fact, I often wonder how many of the adults in the worship services of existing churches think of the services as "boring" church.

This phenomenon causes us to look at two issues. First, much of what we do in our worship services can be uninteresting to children (and many adults) because most worship services only rely on one or two senses—the auditory and the visual. Much of what is said in a sermon can be well over the children's heads intellectually. Keeping children out of the worship service lets us ignore these issues—issues that might very well be tripping points for our adults as well. I also find that the exclusion of children from community worship is rarely replaced with any training, teaching, or experiencing of what happens in corporate worship. In most churches what passes for children's worship is either just an extension of Sunday school with more songs or an entertainment-based hour made into worship simply by naming it so.

Churches desiring to be inclusive in worship need to rethink how their worship services are structured in order to use more of the senses and to incorporate rites and rituals that have meaning across generations. Adults tend to underestimate what children can take away from adult worship services even when little or no attempt is made to be more child friendly. Many parents I meet are convinced that when their children sit in corporate Sunday morning worship, their minds become totally void of any intellectual functioning. But for most children this is simply not the case. Stories abound about children who, when given a pencil and paper to doodle on during the sermon, don't draw superheroes or play hangman but instead draw symbols and representations of what was read from Scripture or what is being said in the sermon.

As those responsible for the soul care of the community's children, we need to be teaching children about worship and helping them to understand the rites and rituals of our particular traditions so that when they are included in corporate worship, they know what is going on. Even the youngest children can understand that there are times to be quiet and times to sing and times to say "amen."

Every Sunday at my church our preschoolers are involved in a worship time during their age-segregated education time. They sing; they pray for things that concern themselves and their families; they give gifts to God; they experience silence; and they learn about the ways our church has chosen to conduct our worship of God. During Advent they wait for Christmas (just like the adults do) by marking time with the candles on the Advent wreath. They understand that the cloth on the table is purple because we celebrate the royalty of the coming Christ Child. During Lent they participate in a special giving project because Lent is a time of almsgiving.

During their education time our grade-school children learn about and participate in other parts of worship such as the Call to Worship and Confession of Sin. They recite the day's Psalter and talk about what the words mean. Like the preschool children, they worship according to the seasons of the church year and are able to explain to others that when the cloth on the table is green, it's a time at church when we work hard at growing in our faith in God.

Hopefully when these children are included in our community's weekly worship, they will recognize these rites and rituals and be able to participate in them as readily as the adults who surround them.

The second issue that churches need to address is the larger trend of desiring worship to be entertaining and fun. Somehow the North American church has moved away from seeing worship as something active people of faith give back to God because God is worth worshiping. Instead we seem to understand worship to be a show about God that engages and entertains us and perhaps allows us to walk out the door with an answer to one of life's many dilemmas. Parishioners often choose churches based on how winsome and entertaining the corporate worship is.

I'm not saying that the worship of God ought not to be engaging. Of course it should. Entering into the mystery and majesty of God through praise, prayer, silence, generosity, and interaction with God's voice should perhaps be the most engaging activity one does all week. Worship should never be boring. But being meaningfully engaged in an activity is different from being entertained. In the first we are active participants. In the second we are passive observers. Sometimes worship is difficult. We don't want to praise God or hear God's voice. Sometimes worship grabs us by the nape of the neck and shakes us up as we come face to face with an ineffable God. Sometimes worship is comforting as we bow down before a God who loves us and gave up everything for us. Sometimes worship is joyous as we praise God who does great things for our world. And sometimes worship is all those things at once. Worship should never be a passive experience, and it is never about us.

So when a child says that church is "boring," what that child means is that church is not entertaining in the way a video game, television show, or soccer game is entertaining.

But as the church rethinks community worship as something we give to God and not something the church gives to us in the way of free Christian entertainment, our children will grow up understanding true engagement in the worship of God. Only then will worship become the important piece of their spiritual formation that it is meant to be.

Church with Children

The first and perhaps most difficult step toward involving children in the corporate worship of a faith community is convincing the community, particularly parents, that this is an important part of faith formation. When I first proposed the idea of including children in our corporate worship, my ideas received a largely positive response from people in their 50s and older. I think this is because when these people had young children, most churches did include children in their worship services. It was simply a given that children would be there. The exclusion of children from public worship is a relatively new phenomenon.

Some people e-mailed me, worrying that children would be running amok in the worship area and disrupting their worship. I did my best to assure them that this would not happen (and it hasn't). But interestingly the people who have been most critical of including children in corporate worship are the parents of these children. Some simply refuse to attend church when the children are included in the worship services because there is nothing for their children to do on that Sunday. And despite lots of evidence to the contrary, parents have a difficult time believing that their children "get anything" out of being involved in the worship service. Others believe their worship is disrupted when they are required to parent their children during the worship service.

But these detractors and negative responses should not deter those church leaders invested in the soul care of children. People need to be brought along in their understanding of the scope of corporate worship. They need to experience the inclusion of children in worship in order to dispel myths and see the community functioning together in worship. Through her organization Congregations in Bloom: Children at Worship, Fairless offers a kit for churches to use that will help them pave the way and plan for the inclusion of children in their worship services. It's important to explain to the community that children will be included in worship, and it's important to explain to them the reasons why this is a vital piece of a child's spiritual formation. But at some point churches just need to forge ahead, implement the inclusion of children in worship, and deal with the opposition as it comes along.

If communities are to effectively include children in their worship of God, they need to review the form and content of their worship and the attitudes toward worship in the community. If community members do not understand the worship of God to be a vital piece of their own spiritual formation, it will be hard for them to understand how this is a vital piece of spiritual formation for their children. If community members believe their own church's corporate worship is boring and unaffecting, then they will never believe their children will be attracted to what happens in the worship service.

Churches need to examine why we do certain things in our worship services. It is because they are meaningful and enhance the worship of God, or are they done simply because they've always been done that way? Are we resistant to change the style of a portion of the worship service because it would upset too many people? Churches need to determine which parts of our worship services have become false gods and sacred cows to the members of the community. We need to ask the question, "Has our worship style become a god to our community instead of simply being a process, a vehicle for coming before God and worshiping God?"

In many ways worship is a telling and retelling of God's story to the faith community week after week. And many churches tell the story in the same way week after week. Considering the inclusion of children in our worship services casts a harsh light on our trite and banal ways of telling people the most wonderful story of all. Including children in our corporate worship will compel us to be creative and innovative and fresh with the ways we tell God's story and our story of life with God.

Prior to Easter of last year, filmmakers at Ecclesia, an emerging church in Houston, Texas, filmed the children of the community as they portrayed the events of the story of Easter. This film was edited with the professional skill of independent filmmakers, and the community viewed the film during Easter worship. Apparently the film was such a powerful rendition of the story of Christ's death and resurrection that the pastor of the community was not sure he had anything left to say after the film was shown! Churches who include children in their corporate worship will need to consider who tells the story, remembering that clergy are not always the most gifted and creative storytellers.

One of our church's experiments with transgenerational worship has been having older elementary children act out a passage of Scripture rather than having it read. Not only does this approach engage many of the children physically and experientially, but it engages adult worshipers as well. We also employ children as lectors on a monthly basis. They are asked to read portions of the Scripture lessons for that particular Sunday, thus sending the message that leading worship and participating in worship are tasks suited to all ages.

Another question churches will need to grapple with when including children in weekly worship is how the sermon will be preached and who will do it. Including all generations in corporate worship may mean that a traditional, lecture-style sermon is not preached every Sunday. It may mean that the sermon is enhanced with visuals. The use of video and still pictures during the sermon can heighten understanding of the words and attract the attention of young worshipers. At the Ecclesia community in Houston, artists illustrate the biblical exposition of the speaker while it is happening. This technique holds children's attention as they watch to see what the final outcome of the picture will be.

Meaningful inclusion of children in weekly community worship may mean that the sermon time becomes an interactive experience for the congregation rather than a passive, auditory, cognitive experience. It may mean that the sermon is not always at the end of the worship hour. Changing the context and techniques of the sermon may be one of the most difficult things for a community to accept because many churchgoers have been convinced erroneously that worship is all about the intellectual and verbal exposition of a Bible passage with a three-point application that will make one's life better. I've often heard parishioners describe all that comes before the sermon as simply the preliminaries.

Other parts of the worship service will need to be considered and perhaps changed as well when children are included in community worship. Worshipers may need to change their attitudes about the appropriateness of noise and movement during worship services as children are allowed to move around to get a better view of what is happening or simply to get the wiggles out. And children can be taught to understand that there are times to be silent during worship and times when it is okay to make noise—such as when we sing, say "amen" in response to a prayer, or greet each other during the passing of the peace. Sometimes audio cues such as ringing a bell prior to a time of silent confession of sin are helpful to remind children of a time of silence. When the inclusion of children in community worship is accepted by the community parents, other members of the community will learn to take responsibility for helping a child understand appropriate behavior during certain parts of a worship gathering or help the child follow the order of service in the bulletin. If a child becomes particularly fidgety or restless during a worship service, parents should be responsible to remove the child.

Changes may need to be made in how children are seated during the worship service. Parents are often inclined to sit with their children as far back in the worship space as possible, believing that disruptions caused by their children will be less noticeable. However, children will be more engaged in the activities of the worship service if they are seated closer to the front where they can see what's happening. If all a child can see is the back of the pew or the head of the person seated in front of him, he is more likely to become bored quickly.

Solomon's Porch in Minneapolis invites school-age children to come and sit up front during the Bible message each week. Sometimes they are invited to participate in quiet activities that reflect the theme or topic of the message. A special area replete with pillows and beanbag chairs is set aside for preteens and teenagers. More formal churches may set up activity areas outside their worship space where children, particularly the younger ones, can move when sitting in the worship service gets to be just too much for them. Parents need to be assured over and over again by the worship leaders and clergy that this movement and noise is totally acceptable to the worshiping community.

Preparing children for what they'll experience during the worship service can greatly aid the child's interest in and understanding of the worship experience. Most churches that use weekend bulletins print them a few days prior to the start of the worship services, so I encourage parents to pick one up at the church building prior to their attendance at worship. They can then walk through the events of the worship experience with their children, discussing why each activity is included in the service and perhaps challenging the children to listen for certain things to be said or to watch for certain things to be done. During the worship service parents can prompt children quietly to look at certain things that are happening in the front or in other parts of the worship space. Gretchen Wolff Pritchard says—

> For parents, especially, accepting children as fellow worshipers means learning new ways of interacting with them in church. Instead of saying "Shhhhh!!!" or offering a cracker or a bottle or a storybook (even a Bible storybook), we parents will need to learn to invite our children to experience the liturgy with us, on their own level. We will need to sit right in front, where children can see, and to pick up a restless child, and gently whisper in his ear, "Look, do you see the priest? What is she doing? Listen, now she's going to say some special words that Jesus said...See, now she's picking up the cup..."[4]

Those who are officially in charge of the soul care of children in the community of faith can teach children about worship during those age-segregated education times that are a part of most children's ministries.

At my church we use the liturgical colors to teach our children about the liturgical year during Sunday school and midweek programming. We teach the children about the various parts of the worship service so they will understand why we pray at the beginning of the service, why we confess our sins, and why we read Psalms together. Some of the litanies and prayers used during our children's worship have been incorporated into our community worship services when the children are included so the children find something in the service that is familiar to them.

Inclusive Worship

On one particular Sunday we had the children move en masse twice during our corporate worship. There were two women sitting on either side of one of my children's ministry volunteers. When the children moved the second time, one grumbled about having children in the worship service, and the other commented on how wonderful it was to have the children worshiping with us. These two attitudes represent both ends of the spectrum you'll encounter when you begin to talk about involving the whole community in the corporate worship of God!

Fairless reminds us that the point is to include children, to help them to feel they are equal participants in the community's worship of God. It is not simply about accommodating children—or adults.[5] The mentality of accommodation suggests that we need to do something *for* the children rather than saying we need to do something with them. Traditional children's sermons are a good example of accommodating children during community worship rather than including them.

Most churches incorporate children's sermons into their worship services because they think they need to pause in their worship to do something for the children. But most children's sermons do little to engage the community as a whole. If a church is going to include children's sermons as part of their transgenerational worship, they need to think about how they can use these times to involve more than just the children. For example, a children's "sermon" can be as simple as including children in other parts of the worship experience. When we have infant baptisms during our worship times, we invite the children to come up front and sit on the steps in front of the baptism participants. This gives the children an opportunity to move about during the service and gives them front-row seats for the baptisms. It makes them participants and reminds the congregation of the vow they make during baptisms to care for all the children of the community.

On another occasion our senior minister invited all the children to come up to the front of our Meeting House for a tour of our worship space. He took them up into the pulpit, explaining to them that our theological tradition requires the minister to speak God's Word from above the people. He gathered them around the communion table and talked about what happens there when we celebrate the Eucharist. Now, while he was speaking explicitly to the children, he didn't dumb down his language for them. That made it possible for the worshiping adults to feel included and, perhaps, learn as much as the children did.

When I participate in a traditional children's sermon, I'm very careful not to fall into the trap of using symbolic language and abstract ideas. While the adults love the traditional object lesson, most children never make the connection between the nifty science experiment and the spiritual truth it's supposed to represent. Therefore, I use the children's sermon to retell the biblical narrative on which the sermon is based. I might bring in pictures or objects that help illustrate that retelling, but I don't use allegory or symbolism. If it's a special day or holy season of the church year, I talk with the children about that season or day, again bringing in something for them to look at, touch, smell, or take home that illustrates the meaning of the season.

Sometimes I choose to involve the whole congregation in the children's sermon. For example, during a children's sermon on the first Sunday of Advent, I invited the children to shout as loud as they could, "Jesus is coming!" Then I challenged the adults in the room to join with the children in shouting as loud as they could, "Jesus is coming!" And they did it! Adults don't often get a chance to shout as loud as they can in church worship services, and they clearly enjoyed it.

I am convinced that at the heart of the resistance to the complete inclusion of children in corporate worship is that adults, particularly parents, don't really think children get anything important out of the worship experience. Parents believe that the potential hassle of having their children with them during worship outweighs the minimal benefit to their children. On a Sunday-by-Sunday basis that might be true. But just as few adults are formed by a single worship experience, children also need the opportunity to stick with inclusive worship before we can measure its impact on them.

One mom from Solomon's Porch in Minneapolis told me she was beginning to doubt that her children were really benefiting from their inclusion in worship. Then one night she was helping two of her boys get ready for bed. The younger of the two asked her what heaven is like. Before she could answer, the boy's brother said something like this, "Chico, you know what heaven is like. It's just like that song we sing at church." And with that Reuben recited the words to "Streets of Gold," a song written by the Solomon's Porch community that is indeed about heaven! This young boy's spiritual understanding of life with God in heaven was richer for being included in the community's worship. This mom is now convinced that including children in worship is actually an important step in their spiritual development. It's important for the church, too.

The nurture of children in the parish is much more than Christian Education. Children learn by watching and imitating adults, and by projecting themselves into imaginary worlds. Our liturgy, with its rich mixture of verbal and non-verbal, of colors, sounds, smells, and gestures, is the primary source of nourishment for our adults, and it should nourish our children as well. But if this is to happen, clergy and worship committees must give serious thought to making Sunday worship truly accessible to children and educating parents and other parishioners to see children as fellow worshipers, not as intruders who have to be hushed or distracted so that the adults are left free to pray.[6]

Children of any age are never intruders in our corporate worship of God, and I believe it is an affront to God to ever consider them so. Children of this generation and with the generations to come crave experience with God and the people of God. The corporate worship of the community of God's people is meant to be, more than anything else, an experience of God and of our relationship with God.

Notes

1. Westerhoff, John M., *Will Our Children Have Faith?* Harper and Row, 1976, 55ff.

2. Fairless, Caroline, *Children at Worship,* Church Publishing, 2002. (From the Foreword, p. ix, by Louis Weill.)

3. The author is indebted to the work and writing of Caroline Fairless, especially her book, *Children at Worship,* Church Publishing, 2002.

4. Pritchard, Gretchen Wolff, *Offering the Gospel to Children,* Cowley Publications, 1992,143-144.

5. Fairless, 9.

6. Pritchard, 143.

nine

Postmodern Faith Formation

One of my current children's ministry volunteers said to me in passing a few months ago, "What you are doing [in children's ministry] is definitely counter-cultural, but you need to keep doing it."

There is a growing sense in our churches that something needs to change if we are to meet the spiritual needs of children in our rapidly changing postmillennial culture. First and foremost, churches need to rethink their current means and trends of ministry to children. At the end of the 20th century, churches were seduced by the sirens of consumerism. They came to believe that providing Disneyesque children's programs constituted the path to larger adult attendance numbers. In doing so they disregarded and lost a sense of what it means to spiritually form children and help children know and love God and live in the way of Jesus. They lost a sense of what children need spiritually from the adults in their lives.

None of these changes will come easily. Some parents don't like it when we include children in our worship services, so they refuse to attend church on the Sundays we do this. A nearby modern church has what is seen as a vibrant children's program with lots of kids, and there are parents in my church who want us to be them. I hear complaints when I don't offer children's programs to support adult programs or when I require parents to come to certain parts of a program so they can learn together with their children. I've had to fight more fights in this ministry situation than in any other church I've served. But on most days I continue to think the fight is worth it because I believe I am fighting for the souls of children and for a community that has the potential to be the light and salt Jesus talked about, particularly in the way it is slowly beginning to value the souls of children.

But my community of faith is not your community of faith. Your battles will be different from mine, and the way your community builds its children's ministry around the three poles of family, community, and worship will look different from the way my community has chosen to do that. I believe firmly that as emerging churches develop their vision for the soul care of their children, these plans, ideas, and innovations will grow out of the ethos of each particular and peculiar community. There will never be a kit available at the local Christian bookstore that provides everything needed for the spiritual nurture of children in the emerging church of the 21st century.

If I've tried to convey anything in the preceding chapters, it's that the spiritual formation of children is never about how many programs a church has or even about the quality of those programs. It is about the attitudes and quality of the people the children interact with and the overall spiritual and relational quality of the community of faith. Please don't take the ideas in this book as a formula or plan for spiritually nurturing your children. I've attempted to provide big-picture ideas and transferable concepts, but how they play out in your community is solely up to you. And I'm excited to hear about the processes each of your communities develops to care for the souls of your children.

This book is the beginning of a conversation, not the end of one. As I travel around the country to speak and dialogue both with people doing children's ministry in existing churches and with those concerned with caring for children in the emerging church, I find they all have a vague sense that something is not quite right in the world of children's ministry. They know that our world and culture demand we do something different, that we need new priorities in the soul care of children, but no one quite seems to know what those priorities are or how to implement them in their current situations.

This book is an attempt to give those people some guidance and some ideas for moving in these new directions, but it is in no way the last word on the subject.

I'm excited to engage in the dialogue that will come as a result of it.

I'm excited to learn the new things you all have to teach me.

Most of all I'm excited to watch the souls of the children in our care reach for the God who loves them.